TAKE IN THE GOOD

Also by Gina Biegel

Be Mindful and Stress Less

TAKE in the GOOD

SKILLS FOR STAYING POSITIVE AND LIVING YOUR BEST LIFE

GINA BIEGEL, MA, LMFT

ILLUSTRATED BY BREANNA CHAMBERS

Shambhala
Boulder
2020

Shambhala Publications, Inc.
4720 Walnut Street
Boulder, Colorado 80301
www.shambhala.com

9 8 7 6 5 4 3 2 1

First Edition
Printed in the United States of America

⊗ This edition is printed on acid-free paper that meets the American National Standards Institute Z39.48 Standard. ♻ Shambhala Publications makes every effort to print on recycled paper. For more information please visit www.shambhala.com.

Shambhala Publications is distributed worldwide by Penguin Random House, Inc., and its subsidiaries.

Designed by Lora Zorian

Library of Congress Cataloging-in-Publication Data
Names: Biegel, Gina M., author.
Title: Take in the good: skills for staying positive and living your best life/Gina Biegel.
Description: First edition. | Boulder: Shambhala, 2020. |
Audience: Ages: 13 and older.
Identifiers: LCCN 2019007668 | ISBN 9781611807714 (paperback)
Subjects: LCSH: Happiness in adolescence—Juvenile literature. | Stress management for teenagers—Juvenile literature. | Mindfulness (Psychology)—Juvenile literature.
Classification: LCC BF724.3.H35 B44 2020 | DDC 152.4/2—dc23
LC record available at https://lccn.loc.gov/2019007668

CONTENTS

INTRODUCTION
A GUIDE TO YOUR WELL-BEING

Marian Wright Edelman, the founder of the Children's Defense Fund, says, "We have pushed so many of our children into the tumultuous sea of life in small and leaky boats without survival gear and compass." So the question is, do we—whether as teens or even adults—have a road map to the skills and tools necessary for well-being, for taking in the good, and for living our best lives? How can we engage in self-care, positive coping skills, or taking in the good if we have never been taught? When do any of us learn the crucial skills for living our best life? It is my belief that mindfulness and taking in the good are the "survival gear and compass" needed for navigating and living your best life.

This book is intended primarily for a teenage audience, but the skills presented herein are not necessarily things that an adult may have already mastered. We can learn these skills to take in the good whether young or old, and once learned, they can be used for a lifetime. They will have a different meaning to you at different stages of your life, but they can be used by anyone from 12 to 112.

For the past fifteen years, my work and focus has been on adapting Jon Kabat-Zinn's adult Mindfulness-Based Stress Reduction (MBSR) program for teens. I created the teen-adapted program, Mindfulness-Based Stress Reduction for Teens (MBSR-T) in 2004. Learning mindfulness and bringing it into your daily life, whether as a teen or an adult, is invaluable.

Origins of "Take in the Good"

This focus on turning toward beneficial experiences and making them a part of ourselves is grounded in the work of Rick Hanson, a neuropsychologist and author who coined the term "taking in the good." In his books and programs, Dr. Hanson has highlighted the brain's negativity bias—it's like Velcro for bad experiences but Teflon for good ones, as he puts it—and developed structured methods that we can use in everyday life to change the brain for the better. With his blessing and support, I have drawn on and adapted his ideas and tools for this book, including those I learned about in his Positive Neuroplasticity Training.

I wish I had learned about mindfulness and these practices when I was a teen.

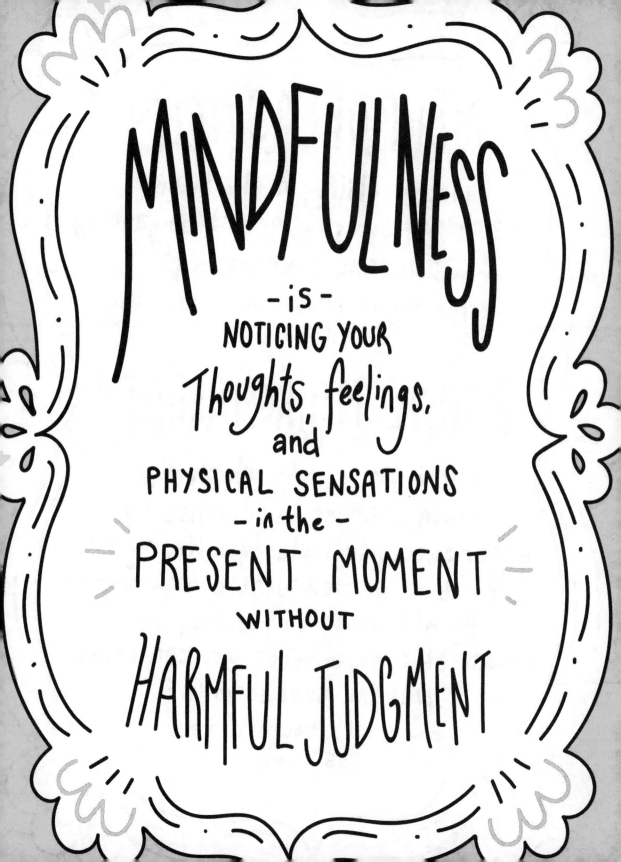

NEUROPLASTICITY

is the ability of the brain to change by creating and reorganizing *NEURAL CONNECTIONS,* especially in response to learning or experience.

POSITIVE NEUROPLASTICITY

is the process by which the brain changes in response to experience, particularly with regard to positive or pleasurable experiences. By attending to positive or pleasurable experiences, you can create *NEURAL CONNECTIONS* that tilt toward the positive.

A GUIDE TO
TAKE IN THE GOOD

Mindfulness helps set the foundations for being able to take in the good because you must be in the present to do so. *Mindfulness* is defined as noticing your thoughts, feelings, and physical sensations in the present moment without harmful judgment. Mindfulness practices help people live in the now by being more present and aware to what is unfolding moment by moment. The intention is that people who are more mindful will focus less on what happened in the past and what is going to happen in the future. This is useful because thoughts on the past or the future are generally connected to worries, ruminations, judgments, doubts, guilt, shame, and the like.

Something I have learned to consider is that once people become more mindful—aware of their thoughts, feelings, and physical sensations—where do they put their attention? Once people are more mindful and aware, what do they do with that newfound awareness and attention? Do they use it to take in the good or do they take in the bad?

The Value of Taking in the Good: The Role of Neuroplasticity

Neuroplasticity is the ability of the brain to change by creating and reorganizing neural connections, especially in response to learning or experience. Leading-edge research on neuroplasticity shows that depending on how the brain is used, the brain can grow approximately fourteen hundred new neurons a day and can create a myriad of new neural connections. The brain continues to change and develop throughout one's life in response to how it is used. These new neurons and neural connections can be harnessed for the good or the bad. You are more likely to attend to the bad because that is the way you are wired.

Due to our evolutionary history, we are wired to fight, freeze, or flee when encountering danger. Though we may not encounter saber-toothed tigers, our brains respond to daily stressors and other traumatic events as if we did. To protect us from harm, our brains are biologically wired to attend to whatever isn't working right, to anything that is bad or negative—this is referred to as the brain's *negative selection bias*. Your brain is more likely to see and focus in on the negative rather than the positive. It can be even harder to harness and take in the good as your brain has evolved to take in the bad. Without deliberate effort and skill, you might perpetuate the natural tendency to focus in on the negative—a taking in of the "bad"—and grow neural connections that further support the negative selection bias.

The good news is that you have the opportunity—every day—to attend to and focus on the good instead of the automatic tendency toward the bad. You can train your brain to focus on and attend to the positive—the act of "taking in the good" to enhance your well-being. *Taking in the good* is the process of noticing, attending to, and taking in a beneficial or "good" experience as it is occurring. We can teach our brains to tilt more to the positive with active training, which is what this book will help you harness. The brain is a sponge, particularly with positive or pleasurable experiences. Research shows us that positive self-talk, thinking, and actions can wash through our brain and shift us away from the negative selection bias. This is why it is so important to actively engage and be present with healthy, positive experiences—so you can learn to construct rather than destruct. By focusing and attending to the positive, you are helping to form positive neuroplasticity.

Positive neuroplasticity is the process by which the brain changes in response to experiences, particularly with regard to positive or pleasurable ones. When we notice, attend to, and take in good, pleasant, and positive moments, we are shifting away from the negative and toward the positive. It takes deliberate effort to notice and recognize good things, and this book provides a map of ways to do just that—to notice, take in, and savor the sweetness life has to offer. Research suggests that—despite our evolution—we can in fact learn how to be more mindful in our lives and then turn that newfound attention toward taking in the good and focusing on the positive.

We have the capacity to see the extraordinary in the ordinary—it is all in the way we choose to look at things and perceive our world. Making this shift in perspective happen isn't always easy, but it can be done. We can train our mind just like we build muscles; we just need to commit to taking the time, putting in the effort, and doing the practice. Using the skills in this book can help. We have the power every day to decide where we want to put our attention and focus. Rick Hanson said, "Taking in the good is not about putting a happy shiny face on everything, nor is it about turning away from the hard things in life. It's about nourishing well-being, contentment, and peace inside that are refuges you can always come from and return to." Give yourself permission to want good things for yourself and to take in the good your life has to offer every single day. It is a healthy thing to want good things for yourself.

How to Use This Guidebook

I suggest that you work through the chapters in the order they are presented. The skills in this book are progressive and build upon one another, and many are tied to you having worked through the previous activities. You can use the road map on the next few pages as an overview to provide for your well-being. This map lays out how to take in the good and live your best life.

In the middle of each page you will see a bird with a ribbon that says *Take in the Good: Take Action*; this is the core of each activity.

To facilitate taking in the good, you need your survival gear and compass to navigate living your best life. You will see a *Take in the Good: Takeaway* and a compass at the end of each activity. The takeaways are quick points to consider for a given activity. The takeaway might include a sentence to help you remember an important point, or it might ask you to do something in your day that can help make an activity more useful and valuable to you. The compass was chosen because each activity guides you toward enhanced and deeper well-being to live your best life.

In each of the four cardinal directions—north, south, east, and west—you will see the following symbols: an anchor, a brain, a flower, and a heart.

The anchor represents the foundations of mindfulness. These include anchoring ourselves in the present moment, being aware of and choosing where to put our attention, noticing our senses, and attending to our grounding focal points. The anchor reminds us that even when we are in a boat and there are lots of waves around us, *stress waves*, when we drop an anchor from our boat, deep below the surface it is calm and still. This anchor helps ground us and gets us to our calm, still place.

The brain represents neuroplasticity and positive neuroplasticity and stands for our becoming more deeply aware of the landscape of our mind—our thoughts and feelings. It reminds us of our ability to change our brain depending on how we use it. We can use our brain to take in the good instead of our natural hardwiring that tilts us toward the negative.

The flower represents our ability to plant seeds so we can nourish and support ourselves while also pulling weeds— ridding ourselves of things that drain and deplete us. We can learn to grow flower bouquets as resources for ourselves in hard times, just as we can value the weeds we have in order to learn from them.

The heart represents tuning in to our hearts—getting to our heart space and out of our head space. We can come from an attitude of gratitude, self-compassion, self-love, and self-care. We can get to know what our needs are—both basic and fundamental, and work at getting those needs met.

I offer you compassion, blessings, and love on this journey of growth, discovery, and living well.

I leave you with this quote I heard from my colleague Talya Vogel, "We have to know where we are in order to know where we want to go!"

Warmly,
Gina Biegel

THE ROAD MAP TO TAKING IN THE GOOD

FIRST
You Need:
SURVIVAL GEAR
and a
COMPASS

SURVIVAL GEAR
+ COMPASS
LEADS TO
AN OVERALL
SENSE OF

WELL-BEING

WELL-BEING
is achieved
by a
constellation
of different
things.

SURVIVAL GEAR

WELL-BEING COMPASS

WELL-BEING BANK

SELF-CARE

TAKE IN THE GOOD

RESOURCE YOURSELF

THE BANK OF WELL-BEING

WHAT IS PART OF YOUR BANK?

- Do things you enjoy doing
- Engage in self-care activities
- Utilize positive coping skills
- Plant seeds- fill yourself with things that nourish and support you

1 : SENSE AWARENESS

Taking in the good begins with being mindful—or aware of your life as it is unfolding moment to moment. Sensory awareness is an accessible way to be mindful at any given moment. When you notice any of your senses, you are doing so in the present moment and, in turn, being mindful.

Your sense awareness is in operation all the time. All day, every day, you are noticing, interacting with, and taking in information from one or more of your five senses—smell, sight, sound, touch, and/or taste. You can pick and choose which you attend to and which you don't.

Research on neuroplasticity suggests that if you attend to something positive for approximately thirty seconds, six to nine times a day, you can facilitate positive neuroplasticity and tilt your brain toward the positive and away from the automatic tendency to the negative—the negative selection bias. Therefore, it can serve you well to pay closer attention to your senses and take in the sensations that improve and enhance your well-being and give less attention and brain time to those that drain or deplete you. Take the time to notice and attend to your senses, to take in all you can, to savor the sweetness of life's moments.

Engaging in positive neuroplasticity doesn't require you to spend extra time seeking out the positive. All you have to do is notice what is already there in your environment, staying mindful of your senses. From the minute you wake up, think of all the opportunities you have to notice different senses in your environment, of those things that nourish and support you—for example, the warmth of a blanket, the smell of something in the kitchen, the look of your pet greeting you in the morning, the sun peeking through your window coverings, and so on. You have a myriad of opportunities day in and day out to use your senses to harness a focus on those things that are pleasant, positive, and useful to you. Noticing your senses in this way, you facilitate taking in the good and engage your brain in positive neuroplasticity.

Take in the Good: Take Action

In this activity, take the time to notice your senses and intentionally choose what you want to attend to. Use the prompts that follow to write about your experiences in the spaces provided on the activity page.

SMELL: If you can, go and smell something you like—a flower, perfume/cologne, honey, coffee, and so on. What was it like to smell something you enjoy?

SIGHT: Take the time to see something you like—favorite photos, nature outside, or a pet playing. What did you notice when you took the time to see something that is pleasant to you?

SOUND: Go and listen to one of your favorite songs or podcasts. How did you feel listening to something that you like?

TOUCH: Feel something you like the touch of—a soft blanket, the fur of your pet, or hug a friend. How do you feel when you touched something you like?

TASTE: Go and taste something you like—fresh fruit, chocolate, tea—and notice what it is like to savor the flavor.

Take in the Good: Takeaway

Part of early learning is to tune in to and be aware of your five senses. Every moment you get to *choose* what you pay attention to and what your focus is on. Use your senses to pay attention to, and take in, the good moments and give less attention and brain time to those moments that don't support your well-being. Using sensory awareness in this way you are taking in the good and engaging in positive neuroplasticity.

Tuning in to your senses helps you to be mindful and more fully aware of what you are doing as you are doing it—even with your hobbies and interests. Being mindful of your daily activities means paying attention to your senses while you are doing that task. Every time you

engage in a hobby you can bring mindful awareness to it by paying attention to your senses. With deliberate effort and attention, you can make the ordinary part of a hobby extraordinary by noticing it with fresh eyes. Imagine seeing something you have seen one thousand times as if it was the first time. Think about a puppy going for a walk—he goes on the same walk, passing the same flowers, bushes, trees, and signs every single day; and yet each time, he eagerly wags his tail and treats it like an incredible new adventure.

You can tilt your brain to the positive while doing something you enjoy by focusing in on your senses. Being mindful of those hobbies you enjoy, you engage your brain to facilitate taking in the good. In addition to practicing mindful sensing of your hobbies and interests, this activity introduces a powerful

mnemonic device that you can use every day: INFO—Interests, New, Feel, and Observe—increasing the likelihood you will take in the good when you engage in hobbies.

Take in the Good: Take Action

On the next pages, write down four of the hobbies, activities, or interests you have. Deliberately choose to focus on those you like and consider to be enjoyable or pleasurable—dance, sports, music, playing video games, and so on. Now fill in all the different things you can see, smell, touch, taste, and hear when you engage in each of the four hobbies.

You can deepen your experience by using INFO (Interests, New, Feel, and Observe) with each hobby. Ask yourself these questions and write down your answers for each.

INTERESTS: What interests you about the hobby? What brings you happiness, peace, and/or joy when you engage in this hobby?
NEW: Look at this hobby with fresh eyes as if it's the first time you have done it. What's new or different about it? Paying attention to your five senses, what's something you haven't noticed before? Anything new or different that you can pay attention to?
FEEL: What do you feel physically and emotionally when you do this hobby? Do you actually enjoy this hobby?
OBSERVE: What do you observe in your surroundings while you engage in this hobby? What good aspects of this hobby can you really attend to and take in?

Take in the Good: Takeaway

Engage in hobbies, activities, or interests you have that nourish and support your well-being. You can deepen your experience and take in the good by using the INFO practice with each thing you do.

HOBBY:	SEE:	SMELL:	TOUCH:	TASTE:	HEAR:

INTEREST:

FEEL:

NEW:

OBSERVE:

HOBBY:	SEE:	SMELL:	TOUCH:	TASTE:	HEAR:

INTEREST:

FEEL:

NEW:

OBSERVE:

HOBBY:	SEE:	SMELL:	TOUCH:	TASTE:	HEAR:

INTEREST:

FEEL:

NEW:

OBSERVE:

HOBBY:	SEE:	SMELL:	TOUCH:	TASTE:	HEAR:

INTEREST:

FEEL:

NEW:

OBSERVE:

3 : MINDFUL EATING

TAKE A MINDFUL BITE

There are three parts to mindful eating:

1. Know your *reason* or intention for why you are going to eat and what
    you are choosing to eat. Ask yourself these questions: Are you eating
    because you are hungry, sad, wanting a sweet treat, or is it that you
    haven't given it much thought? It is important to tune in to your food
    choices and notice the reason you are eating.
2. Notice *what* you are eating while you are eating it from one bite to an
    entire meal. In this way, you are using food to engage in the aware-
    ness of your senses, thoughts, and feelings. Pay attention to what
    foods you like and dislike, stop eating when you are full, and pause if
    you are doing something else.
3. *How* do you feel after you eat? Check in with yourself. Do you feel
    satisfied, full, stuffed? Did you eat too much, too little? Do you feel
    any unpleasant feelings from eating—maybe you ate because you
    were upset? Or do you feel any pleasant feelings from eating—such as
    savoring the sweetness of what you ate?

Being mindful to as many areas of your life as possible, even to your eating, is useful because:

-   You bring more attention to what is occurring as it's taking place;
-   You reduce your mind's tendency to focus on the past or future and
    place more focus on the now;
-   Increased practice attending to the pleasant and positive aspects of
    the routine things you do, including eating, enhances the likelihood
    that you will do so while you take in the good.

Take in the Good: Take Action

For a mindful eating challenge, each day this week list on the next page which bites of different foods you like and which you dislike. The interesting twist is to find foods you thought you liked that you actually dislike. For example, maybe you ate a chocolate you thought you loved but eating it mindfully you found you don't actually care for it that much.

Take in the Good: Takeaway

It is important to know your reasons for eating, and to pay attention to how you feel while and after you eat. You can learn about how food is affected by your mood and in turn how your mood affects what you choose to eat.

Take a Mindful Bite

MON: LIKES: · DISLIKES:

TUES: LIKES: · DISLIKES:

WED: LIKES: · DISLIKES:

THURS: LIKES: · DISLIKES:

FRI: LIKES: · DISLIKES:

SAT: LIKES: · DISLIKES:

SUN: LIKES: · DISLIKES:

4 : TAKE A BREAK WITH THE 3 BS

BODY, BREATHE, BEGIN

Taking a short break and checking in with yourself from time to time throughout the day is a good habit to develop. It's important to notice how you are doing from one moment to the next because we can get so caught up in our day that we might not even notice how we're doing. For example, by pausing to check in with yourself, you might suddenly notice that you are in fact hungry, tired, or have a headache that has gone unnoticed.

Taking a break with the 3 Bs (Body, Breathe, Begin) helps you check in with yourself. It is valuable to turn inward and listen to what information you are provided. Consider this: You take a break with the 3 Bs and notice that your day is going miserably, and your focus has been on the unpleasant. This realization can guide you to do something quite different. You might choose to shift your perspective by focusing on that which is more enjoyable and pleasant to you. You have power and control every day to decide where you want to put your attention and focus.

Take in the Good: Take Action

Use the four quadrants on the next page to take a break and check in with yourself at four different times today. In the boxes provided next to the symbol for each, record your responses to the prompts below when you check in with the 3 Bs.

1. *BODY:* Notice how you feel in your body. Release and relax any tension. Now, list what you noticed in your body.

2. *BREATHE:* Notice your breath. Pay attention to how you are feeling and what you are thinking. Now, take a deep breath and follow it from the in-breath to the out-breath. Now, list what you are aware of.

3. *BEGIN:* Begin again. Return to whatever you were doing and start anew. Now, list any insights or changes you want to make as you move on to the rest of your day.

Take in the Good: Takeaway

The information the 3 Bs provide can help you to make informed decisions on how to proceed for the rest of your day, which actions you take, and which choices you make.

Take a Break with the 3 Bs

- BODY:
- BREATHE:
- BEGIN:

1.

2.

3.

4.

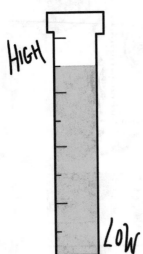

5 : MINDFUL CHECK-IN

YOUR HIGHS AND LOWS

What makes your days meaningful? What were the highs that you can take in and savor to enhance your well-being? What were the low points that maybe you would have preferred not to have happened? Mindfully taking in the day is about noticing all there is to see in the day—both the highs and the lows. When you check in with yourself in this way, you are putting yourself first; you are saying to yourself that how you feel matters. The highs of your day can be noticed, attended to, and, if you want, savored. It is valuable to savor the enjoyable moments of your life, provided they are healthy. The lows of your day can provide you with useful information. For example, perhaps you can learn about what not to do again and which people, places, things, or events don't serve your best interests. All information is information—whether is it a high or a low moment.

Take in the Good: Take Action

At the end of each day this week, use the next page to jot down what the highs and lows were for each day. Now, looking back at your week, do you tend to have more highs or more lows? Were any of your highs also lows? If you had more lows than highs this week, is this common for you, or was it just this week? If you had a lot of lows, are any of them things you can change moving forward? If you can change and do something different to have fewer lows, that is something to consider. For those things you did that you categorized as highs, can you do more of them? For both your highs and lows what information can you glean from them?

On the last note on the page, write down what your highest highs and lowest lows were. If you can, do more of what serves you well and less of what doesn't.

Take in the Good: Takeaway

It is useful to take the time to notice the roses and thorns, the peaches and pits—the highs and lows that make up each day. You get a constant stream of information from the things you experience—some which support your well-being and those things that harm it. Use this information to guide you to the people, places, things, and events to turn toward or away from.

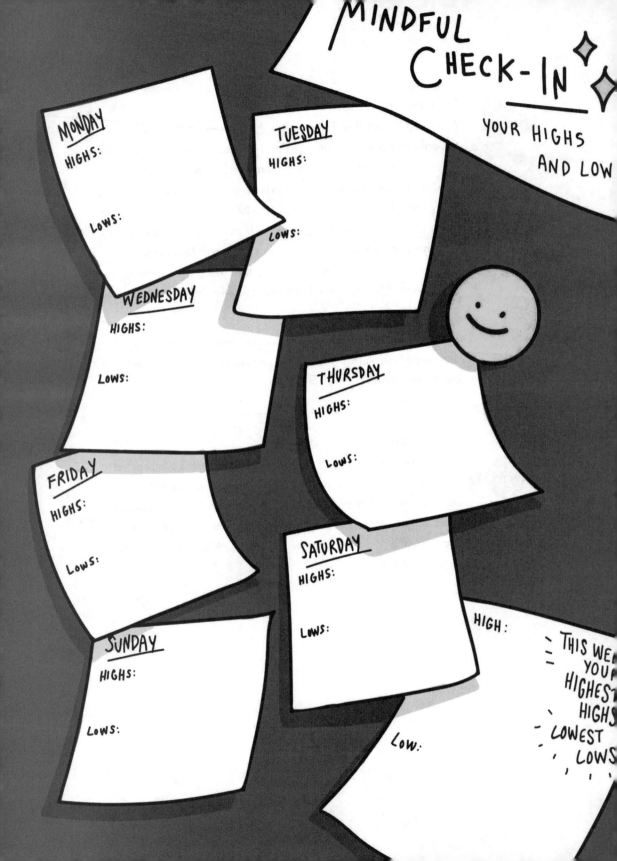

6 : ZOOMING OUT AND ZOOMING IN

SHIFTING YOUR PERSPECTIVE

Y ou have the choice every minute of where you want to put your attention and focus. *Choice awareness* is about choosing where to put your attention. Think about how it's your choice whether to attend to the pleasant or unpleasant. *Spacious awareness* is being aware of what is literally in your space: what is around you in your immediate surroundings, what's in front of you and behind you, and noticing your five senses. Once you are aware of your space, surroundings, and senses, in that moment, you can choose to keep your attention on the entirety of what you see or you can focus in on a piece or part. This is where spacious awareness moves to directed awareness. *Directed awareness* is focusing in on something specific and making the choice to do so.

You can experience your environment by shifting your attention from spacious to directed awareness and vice versa. It would be like zooming out and zooming in. Take, for example, the zoom feature on your phone: you can zoom out and see more of the frame or the landscape, and the entirety of what you can see would be spacious awareness. You can zoom in and pay attention to the details of one thing and that would be directed awareness. You can use your own zoom function to play around with what you choose to notice and pay attention to. If you want, you can shift your perspective by focusing in on those things that are pleasant to you and give less attention and brain time to those things that are unpleasant to you. The choice is yours.

Take in the Good: Take Action

Take the drawings on the next two pages: one is a scene that is zoomed out and focuses on the entire landscape, whereas the other is more zoomed in, focusing on one piece of the frame. Look at both scenarios: What do you notice in both scenes looking at them from these two different perspectives? You can apply shifting your perspective by zooming out and in to the way you see and perceive different scenarios in your life. How you view things depends on how you are feeling and what you are thinking about at any one moment.

Take a situation in your life that has you a bit stuck—it might be with a friend, family member, school, or work. On the *Zooming Out* page, write about the whole situation from other people's points of view and include whatever additional information about it you find relevant. On the *Zooming In* page, write about the situation from your perspective, only looking at your point of view. After you are done, you might still see things the same way you did before, but perhaps you were able to gather additional information or understand different points of view.

Take in the Good: Takeaway

You can play around with shifting your perspective anytime you want and go from zooming out to zooming in. At every moment you have the opportunity to choose how you want to perceive things.

ZOOMING IN

7 : YOUR THOUGHTS IN 1 MINUTE OR LESS

With the busyness of daily life and our being surrounded by technological devices that ping and emit noises that snag our attention, it can be hard to know what you are thinking from minute to minute. It is useful, though, to know what your thoughts are. For example, by tuning in to your thoughts you can hear the way you speak to yourself. Is it kind, gentle, firm, or something else? Attending to your thoughts can provide you with useful information and shed light on the way you view things, whether positive and pleasant or negative and unpleasant. These are just a few of the ways noticing your thoughts can help you. When you begin bringing mindfulness into your life and start doing mindfulness practices, you will often become more aware of your thoughts. You will start to notice the contents of your consciousness. You are thinking all the time, you just might not notice it.

Take in the Good: Take Action

Read the comics on the next two pages and notice the different thoughts the characters are having while practicing mindfulness. During mindfulness practice, and during non-practice times, it is normal and natural to be aware of and have all sorts of different thoughts; all thoughts are allowed, there are no right or wrong thoughts to have, they are just the thoughts you are having.

Now, set a timer for one minute and close your eyes. Note where your mind goes; whatever arises in your mind is what arises in your mind. You will learn more on what to do with thoughts later. For now, just notice them. Lastly, on the final two pages of this activity in the blank comics record the thoughts you remember having regardless of what they were. Some thoughts might seem unimportant such as, "I have an itch" or "Oh, I forgot to do that thing." Regardless, these are still your thoughts, and knowing what you are thinking is very helpful whether insignificant to you or not.

Take in the Good: Takeaway

When practicing mindfulness there are no "perfect" thoughts or thoughts you are supposed to have. Noticing your thoughts is the first step to becoming more aware. Awareness can lead to beneficial positive change.

8 : MINDFUL WALKING AND PHOTOGRAPHY PRACTICE

Walking is something you usually just do without giving it a lot of thought. Unlike most walking where you are striving to get to a specific destination or end point, mindful walking isn't about getting anywhere. Walking mindfully is noticing your body while you walk, tuning in to the act of walking while you are doing it, and using your feet as an anchor to ground you in the moment.

Take in the Good: Take Action

Part I: Take a Mindful Walk for Five Minutes

Set a timer for five minutes, read this part, and then proceed with your mindful walk. Pay attention to how you walk. Notice what walking feels like in your body: lifting your foot, shifting to the other foot, stepping, placing your feet, and repeating. Ground yourself to the moment with every step you take. When you pay attention to your feet, you are in the present moment, not in your head focusing on your to-do list, worries, judging this or that, and so on. You get a mental time-out when you mindfully walk. Thoughts will arise and things will get noticed. If that happens, just pause your walking and notice what you got distracted by—a thought, something you saw, a noise—and continue walking. When you are finished, write down on the path the different things you remember noticing—any thoughts or feelings or anything that caught your attention.

Part II: Mindful Walking and Photography Practice for Five Minutes

While you mindfully walk you can practice spacious and directed awareness—to decide what to look at and where to put your attention. You can play around with zooming out and in with your camera or cell phone. In this practice, you can choose to attend to things that are pleasant and beneficial or to those things that are unpleasant and unhelpful. Now, for five minutes, mindfully walk and bring your camera or cell phone. This time when you get distracted by something you see, stop, attend to whatever it was you noticed, and take a picture of it. You might even try zooming out and in on the same thing to play around with where you put your attention and how you can shift your perspective on the same thing. Take at least four pictures of things that catch your attention, and make sure you take one picture of something that is odd, out of place, or just doesn't seem to fit. Take at least five pictures all told. When you are done, record what pictures you took on the lines next to the cameras on the next page, and beneath the last camera on the tripod, describe the picture you took of something that didn't fit or belong.

Mindful walking can help get you out of your head by using your feet to ground you to the moment. Taking pictures while walking adds an element of experimenting with where you put your attention and playing around with shifting your perspective.

Take in the Good: Takeaway

When you want to increase the juju of your day, consider taking a mindful walk noticing what interests you and catches your attention. You can choose to take a walk where you know you enjoy the views or go and create a beneficial experience by finding a new place to walk. You can even take pictures to capture the moment to help savor it.

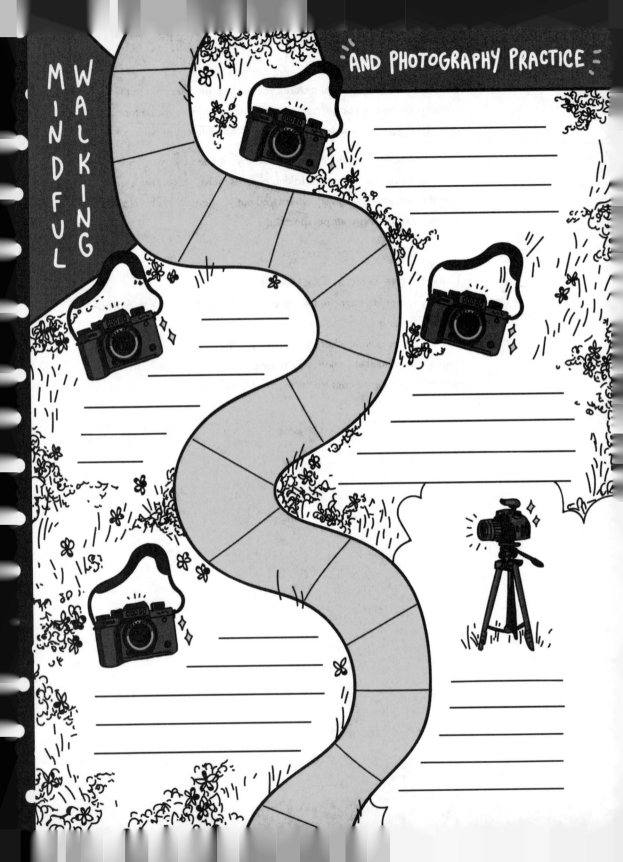

9 : GROUNDING FOCAL POINTS

You have the power, every moment, to shift how you are feeling and what you are thinking. Attending to a bodily constant—a.k.a. "grounding" yourself—can help you tolerate and get through hard moments mindfully. When in physical or emotional pain, people tend to automatically react by pushing away or clinging to the pain. Grounding helps you to mindfully be with the experience as it is occurring and not add to or detract from the pain. Noticing your *grounding focal points*—fingers, hands, breath, heart, and feet—can help. For example, if you are having an awful day, you can turn to any one of these focal points as a way to get out of your head and help "ground" yourself in the present moment. Notice how these physical points help connect your mind and body. When things are difficult, being able to ground yourself is a great skill to have in your survival gear to help you get through difficult moments that are part and parcel of life. On the other hand, if you are having a wonderful day, you can notice any one of these focal points to help you really absorb, savor, and take in the good of the moment by connecting to this experience deeply—not just in your mind but also in your body.

TAKE IN THE GOOD: TAKE ACTION

On the next page, look at the examples of each of the grounding focal points. Now go and focus in on each of these points and write about your experiences in the circles provided on the following page. Use the prompts below to help you take a deeper dive into your experience.

- Intentionally go and touch something you like to feel and take the time to notice and savor what it feels like on your *fingers* and *hands*.
- Do something to change your breathing and heartbeat; maybe engage in a physical activity, dance around, or sing along to a song and notice how your *breath* and *heart* change.
- Notice something under your *feet*—a different surface or texture. If you can, go barefoot to feel the ground under your feet—walk on grass, sand, or even in water.

TAKE IN THE GOOD: TAKEAWAY

Grounding focal points—your fingers, hands, breath, heart, and feet—help connect your mind and body. When going about your daily routine, notice any of these to change how you are feeling or enhance the experience of any moment.

Just as it is important to know what your thoughts are, it is important to know what your stressors are. Even when you aren't actively paying attention to your thoughts or stressors, they are affecting your physical and emotional well-being. Knowing what is causing you stress provides you information that you can use to set your course for well-being. Imagine the waves in the ocean representing everything that is causing you stress right now: your *stress waves*—many stressors, many waves; few stressors, few waves. Just as you can't stop the waves, you can't stop stress from coming, but what you can do is to choose how you want to handle and manage these stress waves.

TAKE IN THE GOOD: TAKE ACTION

In the box on the next page draw your "stress waves." Label the waves with the stressors (events, worries, fears, problems, concerns, and the like) that created these waves. After you do this consider the following questions: Are your waves, big, small, mean, fierce, calm, mellow? Are there any patterns to your waves, for example, around the same person or theme? What thoughts or feelings come up for you when you look at the stressors you listed?

Doing this activity can at times create heightened stress or anxiety. Remember, when you find yourself stressed, turn to your grounding focal points—those physical constants such as your feet or fingers that can help ground you in this moment. Although this can be hard, it is very important to know explicitly what is stressing you out because then you can take action to work on your stressors to change the level of stress they cause you. These stressors were there before you wrote them down, you were just holding them inside; now that they are explicit you can do something about them and don't have to take the mental energy and space to hold them inside.

TAKE IN THE GOOD: TAKEAWAY

Making your stressors explicit (writing them down) can help you create an action plan of what to tackle first. Now you can actively do something about your stressors rather than being a passive observer of them.

11 : RIDE THE WAVES

MANAGE YOUR STRESS

Knowing what is stressing you out is the first part of managing and dealing with your stress. Learning which of these stressors are (1) manageable (you can actually enact change), (2) not easily manageable (you can change with some work), or (3) unmanageable (difficult to change) is the second part. The last part is to make changes where possible—the skills you learn in this book can help you become more able to tolerate, manage, and deal with your stressors.

Take in the Good: Take Action

Complete this activity using your responses from the last activity, *Your Stress Waves*, and add any other stressors that come to mind or that you want to include. Place your stressors in the category in which they best fit.

The first category on the next page is for *Short-Term, Acute, or Manageable Stressors*. Write down any and all stressors that you can do something about to change them right now. It is suggested that you manage these first. These are stressors that you can do something about, that are fixable, or can be changed. Working on these first can provide you with incremental success in managing your stressors. This can help you feel some immediate relief. Reducing these stressors makes dealing with the more difficult and enduring ones more doable.

For the middle category, *Long-Term, Chronic, or Not Easily Manageable Stressors*, list those stressors that are more permanent, inflexible, or difficult to change. In the last category, *Enduring or Unmanageable Stressors*, list those stressors that can't change. These might be due to the fact that what is causing you stress happened in the past and can't be undone. Such a stressor might involve other people's actions or situations that are out of your control. Finally, it might be something health related that can't be undone. These are just a few of the examples of stressors that can't change. How you react to and handle them is in your control.

Going through this process and listing these stressors lets you know what they are, which ones you can change, which ones might take some work but can still change, and which are the ones that can't change. You also know now that these stressors are listed on paper, you don't have to hold on to them tightly and give extra mental energy to them. You can attend to and work on those manageable stressors and make the changes you can. Work on the more long-term stressors when you are able to and can tolerate managing them. Lastly, work to change how you react and handle those that are out of your control. The following activities are here to guide and help you manage your life stressors and increase your well-being.

Take in the Good: Takeaway

Like waves, your stressors will come and go and change from day to day. It is important to remember that even when things are most difficult in your life, this too shall pass. Don't forget you can weather the storm—the waves will pass. You can ride a surfboard over the waves!

Ride the Waves: Manage Your Stress

SHORT-TERM, ACUTE, or MANAGEABLE SRESSORS:

LONG-TERM, CHRONIC, or NOT EASILY MANAGEABLE STRESSORS:

ENDURING or UNMANAGEABLE STRESSORS:

12 : DROP ANCHOR

Look at the image of the rowboat on the activity page and follow the anchor down to the ocean floor. This anchor holds the boat in place when waves are ebbing and flowing. Additionally, when the anchor is deep below the surface of the water, even if the surface has fierce and strong waves, the ocean floor is mostly calm and still. Imagine yourself having anchors that can hold you in place and help you to drop down below your stress waves to your calm and still place.

Take in the Good: Take Action

Tips on things that can help you drop anchor just from the skills you have already learned in this book:

- Pay attention to any of your five senses
- Engage in a hobby or activity you enjoy
- Take a break with the 3 Bs
- Take a mindful walk
- Zoom out or in to shift your perspective
- Pay attention to your grounding focal points

On the next page, in the lines numbered from 1 to 10, list any and all people, places, things, or situations that help:

- Support you
- Ground you
- Reduce your stress
- Encourage your strengths
- Center and/or calm you

Engage with the people, places, things, or situations that either support and help anchor you in your stress waves and get you to your calm, still place, or else help you as you work to manage and change your stressors.

Take in the Good: Takeaway

You can use any of these resources to help anchor you when life gets difficult and stressful. Remember, even if the surface of the ocean has fierce, pounding stress waves you can drop anchor to your calm and still place.

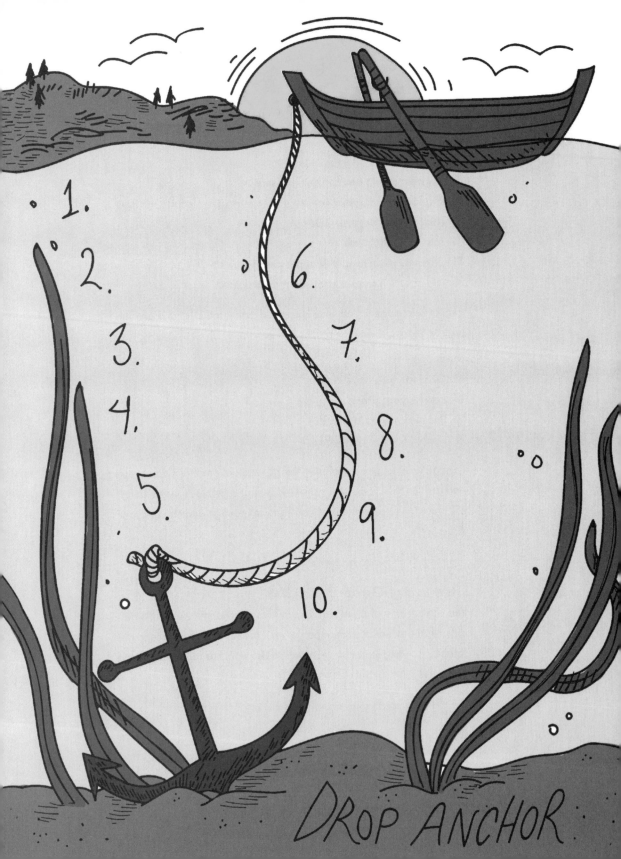

13 : DROPPING-IN MINDFULNESS PRACTICE

When you are stressed out, focusing on, or working to manage your stress waves it can be useful to engage in a short mindfulness practice to help you to literally "drop in" to this moment. By doing this short practice, you can tune in to what you are thinking and how you are feeling—physically and emotionally. This is a literal drop-anchor activity because you are taking the time to arrive and be in the moment just as it is now.

Take in the Good: Take Action

Read about the practice on the next two pages first, then set your timer and do the practice for five minutes.

When you have completed the practice, use the third activity page, the *Mindfulness Practice Debrief*, and answer the prompts in the four quadrants:

- Did you encounter any barriers or obstacles during the practice? Listing these can provide you with information about things you might want to change next time you engage in this or any other mindfulness practice. You can use this debrief anytime you do a mindfulness practice—even the walking practice.
- What thoughts and feelings do you remember having during your practice? Include those that stand out to you the most.
- What did you notice as you attended to your body? This section is having you tune in more to your physical experience during your practice—pains, itches, discomforts, sensations, parts of your body going to sleep, and so on.
- Write about any awareness, insights, or "aha" moments you had during the practice that you remember.

Take in the Good: Takeaway

Drop in to this moment. Once you become more aware of your body, breath, and mind—including the thoughts and feelings that arise— you can make needed changes or focus on anything that is potentially beneficial or useful to you and less on that which is potentially harmful to you.

DROPPING-IN MINDFULNESS PRACTICE

Allow yourself to DROP IN TO THIS MOMENT, just as it is. You are not trying to get anywhere and there is nothing to attain. This practice is about noticing what is, as it is, and settling into this moment. You can use it to drop down below the stress waves of your life to get to your calm, still place, like an anchor released from a boat. This practice is an offering of *self-care* — because you are taking time for yourself. Do it for your own benefit, not for anyone else's.

TIPS

• BEFORE YOU BEGIN

Minimize any distractions; turn off your cell phone and other technology or put them on silent. Read through these guided instructions first, and then get into a comfortable position, seated or lying down. Adjust everything until you get to a "Yes, I'm comfortable" position. Readjust yourself during the practice if needed.

Once you have read the instructions, start a timer for five minutes, and begin the practice.

GUIDED INSTRUCTIONS

• NOTICE YOUR MIND: THOUGHTS AND FEELINGS •

During this practice, just notice thoughts and feelings as they arise. You can say to yourself, Then you can return to where you were before.

"oh, interesting. This is what I'm thinking and feeling right now."

Your mind will have thoughts and feelings. It is normal and natural to have these; that's what minds do. Witness whatever arises—thoughts and feelings can provide you with information. It is valuable to know the contents of your consciousness instead of going along on automatic pilot.

Notice your thoughts as you would the ticker at the bottom of a television screen; just watch them go by. Remember, just because you have a thought doesn't mean you have to believe it to be true, real, or factual. Once you notice a feeling, just welcome it as a visitor; like a visitor, its presence is temporary, not permanent.

• NOTICE YOUR BODY AND BREATH

Scan your body from the tips of your toes moving up to the top of your head. Notice any points of contact your body has with what you are sitting or lying on.

Notice your toes and feet; if they are surrounded by socks or shoes, just notice that. Use your toes and feet to be a beginning anchor to this moment as you work your way up to the top of your head.

Notice any pains or physical sensations that are present along the way. You might notice something new, you might notice something familiar—like a detective, just notice what is here to be observed. Welcome any pains and physical sensations; like waves, they will come and go.

If you notice a pain or sensation, you can breathe into any area you choose. Perhaps consider bringing in cool, clean, fresh air on your next in-breath and releasing any tension on your next out-breath.

Notice both of your feet, legs, and hips as you move to your stomach and chest. Notice your ribs and lungs expanding and releasing as you breathe. You can also place one or both hands on your heart and notice your heart beating.

Move your attention down to the tips of your fingers and your hands. Notice the air that surrounds them; feel any sensations present here. Notice your lower back and spine as you move up to your neck and the back of your head and face.

Let go of any tension you are holding in your body. Your shoulders are a great place to check; if they are tight, consider releasing them and letting your arms float like kelp in the ocean. Now notice if you are holding a facial expression; if your teeth or jaw is clenched, release it. If you are holding your lips in a fixed position, release them. There is no need to hold any position right now.

MINDFULNESS PRACTICE DEBRIEF

ANY **BARRIERS** or **OBSTACLES** YOU WANT TO WORK TO PREVENT OR DECREASE NEXT TIME?

EXAMPLES:

> Quieting distractions
> Knowing your breath changes when you notice it

WHAT DID YOU NOTICE IN YOUR **MIND**: YOUR **THOUGHTS** AND **FEELINGS**?

WHAT DID YOU NOTICE IN YOUR **BODY**? HOW DID YOU TURN TO OR USE YOUR **BREATH**?

ANY **INSIGHTS** YOU WANT TO TAKE AWAY FROM YOUR PRACTICE? ANY **AHA** MOMENTS?

14 : TAKE IN THE GOOD

Doing What You Enjoy

Why don't we engage in activities we enjoy doing regularly if it improves our health and happiness? Do we find we are not deserving of health and happiness? Does it take too long to do something we like to do? When we are tired or feel miserable, this is often the time we don't want to do things that we like even though it will make us feel better. At times it requires deliberate effort to do the things we like, especially when we are feeling stressed, overwhelmed, or down in the dumps.

Every day is full of opportunities to "take in the good" of what you are doing, particularly if it is something you like and enjoy doing. You can have positive experiences by actively doing something you enjoy or by noticing the little things that are pleasant and enjoyable that sometimes go unnoticed—like a smile from a friend or a bird that flies by. When you take in the good and enjoy what you are doing, you are enacting *positive neuroplasticity*.

SMELL THE FLOWERS

TAKE IN THE GOOD: TAKE ACTION

On the list on the next page, mark all of the things that you enjoy doing (use the blank lines to add any others). Now list the top five things you like to do from the entire list at the bottom of the page.

Today, or as soon as possible, engage in one of these things—or more than one—that you like to do.

TAKE IN THE GOOD: TAKEAWAY

There are many opportunities to savor the sweetness of those things you like to do—don't let those moments go by unnoticed and unused. Take in the good and use these moments to your benefit.

TAKE IN THE GOOD

DOING WHAT YOU ENJOY

- [ ] Spending time with pets
  - [ ] Nature/being in the outdoors
- [ ] Writing, journaling, blogging
  - [ ] Internet, social networking, posting
- [ ] Taking pictures
  - [ ] Doing a hobby or craft
- [ ] Playing or listening to music
  - [ ] Spending time with your friends
- [ ] Spending time with your family
  - [ ] Gardening
- [ ] Drawing or painting
  - [ ] Exercising
- [ ] Playing a sport
  - [ ] Dancing
- [ ] Singing
  - [ ] Cooking
- [ ] Building projects
  - [ ] Playing video games
- [ ] Driving
  - [ ] Skiing or snowboarding

- [ ] Mindfulness practice
  - [ ] Doing yoga
- [ ] Reading
  - [ ] Taking a shower or bath
- [ ] Watching movies
  - [ ] Volunteering
- [ ] Eating out
  - [ ] Going to a sporting event
- [ ] Going to a concert
  - [ ] Camping out
- [ ] Traveling
  - [ ] Talking on the phone
- [ ] Going to a mall or shopping
  - [ ] Playing a musical instrument
- [ ] Napping
  - [ ] Nails or hair tutorial
- [ ] Board game night
  - [ ] _____
- [ ] _____

MY TOP 5

1. _____
2. _____
3. _____
4. _____
5. _____

PLEASANT MOMENTS CALENDAR

When people get home at the end of their day, most look back to reflect and find that it was either a good day or a bad day. People don't often notice the different moments that take place throughout the day that made that day good or bad. Instead of being one or the other—good or bad—your day is actually filled with many moments: some pleasant, some unpleasant, some neutral. It is interesting to dive into the moments of your day and see just how many you find to be pleasant—especially when you are deliberately focusing in on those things that bring you happiness, peace, and joy.

Capturing Your Life Moments

Take in the Good: Take Action

For the next week, try noticing and attending to those things that are pleasant to you. By noticing the pleasant moments in your day you can choose to (1) attend to them, (2) take in the good the moment has to offer, and (3) actively focus your time on those things that are pleasant as opposed to those that are unpleasant to you. Unpleasant moments will come, but this week try to notice, attend to, focus on, and zoom in to those pleasant moments in your day.

At the end of each day, reflect back and list one thing that you found pleasant, writing it on the next page in the column titled *Moment*. Then check in with the *Thoughts and Feelings* you have or had about that pleasant moment and list them in that column. Next, tune in to the *Physical Sensations* of your body—what you feel or remember feeling when you think about that pleasant moment—and list them in the third column. Now hold the memory of that pleasant moment in your mind; pay attention to it for thirty seconds to one minute. Notice what you enjoyed about the moment—take it in and savor it. Make a few notes about it under *Now*.

Take in the Good: Takeaway

Paying attention to the pleasant moments is a way to literally take in the good; you can help take a beneficial experience and create a lasting resource and impression on yourself. You can use your pleasant life moments to your advantage by taking in all you can from them, all the good aspects, and use what happiness, peace, and joy you get from them for your well-being.

PLEASANT MOMENTS CALENDAR

PLEASANT	MOMENT	THOUGHTS + FEELINGS	PHYSICAL SENSATIONS	NOW
MON				
TUES				
WED				
THURS				
FRI				
SAT				
SUN				

UNPLEASANT MOMENTS CALENDAR

Are you someone who looks at life as a glass that's half empty or half full? You have the power and control to decide where you put your attention, how you choose to see your life, and whether it's "half full" or "half empty." Days are filled with many moments—some pleasant, some unpleasant, and some neutral. This week you will attend to the unpleasant. The task is to notice the unpleasant things but not give a lot of extra attention or power to them beyond the information they are providing you. Yes, even unpleasant things, pains, and discomforts are providing you with information. And when the unpleasant is quite significant and intolerable, you can learn to fight back and stand up to it by having a pleasant moment counterpoint.

A DAY IN YOUR LIFE

TAKE IN THE GOOD: TAKE ACTION

This week, you will be attending to and noticing that which is unpleasant to you. Even unpleasant moments have value:

- You might not do what was unpleasant again.
- You can consider the context of the situation and potentially not spend time with the people, places, or things that are draining or hurting you and leading to unpleasant moments.
- You can use these unpleasant moments as learning opportunities.

Each day this week, notice something that is unpleasant to you. At the end of the day, list the unpleasant moment in the first column under *Moment* next to the corresponding day of the week. In the next column, *Experience*, list your thoughts, feelings, and physical sensations that came from the unpleasant moment. In the *Pleasant Moment: A Counterpoint* column, think of and list something that was pleasant to you during that same day. It is interesting that even in days where you are focusing on the unpleasant, you can you still notice something nice. Lastly, in the *Now* column, write about your current experience with that unpleasant moment. Sometimes distance and time away from an experience can lessen the intensity of it. If you have had some distance and time away from the unpleasant moment, how has that changed your experience?

TAKE IN THE GOOD: TAKEAWAY

Your day is more than just "good" or "bad." Start to notice all the different moments of your day. By adjusting your perspective, you can see the wide range of your daily experiences. Make the decision to put your time, energy, and mental effort to engage with and take in the pleasant. You can learn from the unpleasant moments and choose to spend less time and energy focusing on them. The choice is yours!

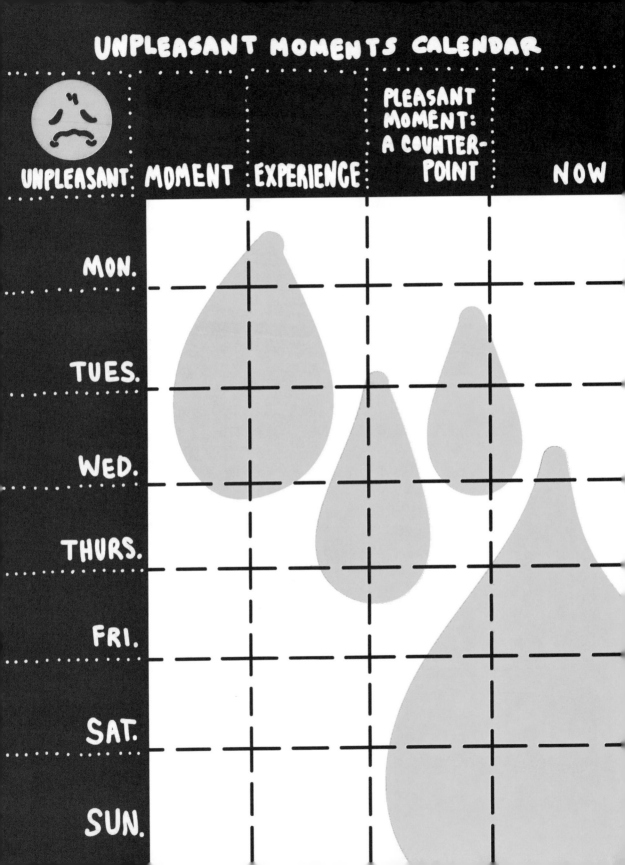

17 : MINDFUL QUALITIES

YOUR VALUES

Mindful qualities help you live your life on your terms with the values and personality traits that are important to you. You can zero in on the qualities that are most important to who you are and how you want to live your life.

Take in the Good: Take Action

The mindful qualities are not listed in order of importance; they are all important and can be more or less significant at different points in your life. Each quality is followed by a short definition or a way to explain or demonstrate it.

Each week, for the next five weeks, you are to pick one of the qualities you want to work on for the week. *Working on a quality* means to notice the presence or absence of the quality in your life each day, at different points throughout your day. These qualities can be directed toward yourself and in most cases toward others—or in your interactions or relationships with others. In addition to noticing the presence or absence of the quality, you can also choose to *use the quality*, that is, put in directed effort to engage with the quality over the week—but it isn't required.

When picking a quality, pick one that fits for something you are working on or dealing with in your life or choose a quality that just stands out to you among the rest, even if you aren't sure why. You can pick the same quality week after week or try a new quality each week—the choice is yours. Even if you are inclined to work on more than one quality a week, only work on one a week.

On page 63, go to the week you are on, from 1 to 5, circle the quality you've chosen for the week and also write it down on the next page under *Chosen Quality for the Week*. To remind yourself which quality you are working on, feel free to cut it out or take a picture of it (I highly recommended this). You can even put reminders on your devices and/ or write the quality on Post-it notes placed around your house or in your bag or locker. Sometimes the only way you will notice your quality is when you see it on the reminders you set up for yourself.

Take in the Good: Takeaway

Mindful qualities help you live a life with intention and purpose. These qualities can be a way to shape your values and what is most important to you.

Mindful Qualities

ACCEPTANCE: Acknowledging that things are the way they are and allowing what is to be as it is.

CURIOSITY: A sense of interest and wonder; the desire to explore, learn, and know.

COMPASSION: Sympathy toward distress in oneself or others, and a desire to reduce it.

NONSTRIVING: Being present with what is, as it is. Not having a set of expectations or an attachment to a particular outcome.

AUTHENTICITY: Being true to one's personality, character, values, beliefs, and principles. A genuine expression of your true self.

NOT KNOWING: The freedom to be curious and open to potential learning. The ability to accept that you don't know everything and the willingness to learn as you go.

BEING VERSUS DOING: *Being* takes place in the present moment; you are not focused on the past or future. *Doing* often happens at a faster pace; you are more focused on finishing and often not in the present — too busy in the act of doing something.

NONHARMFUL JUDGING: A judgment can be harmful to yourself or others. When you make a nonharmful judgment, you intentionally take the time to assess whether something is true, factual, or real before assessing a value to it. Staying neutral without evaluating people, places, things, or situations.

GENTLENESS: Mildness of disposition toward yourself or others. An intentional kindness or warmth.

GRATITUDE: Profound appreciation in the moment. Focusing on what is going well and what you have to appreciate and be thankful for.

PRESENCE: Attending to or being aware of yourself or others. Giving time to be there for yourself or others.

LETTING GO: The process of accepting what you cannot change; an act of releasing control.

OPENNESS: The courage and willingness to experience life without barriers and free from concealment.

PATIENCE: The ability to calmly bear and withstand circumstances. The ability to tolerate without opposition, adversity, or difficulty.

FORGIVENESS: Letting go of resentment or claim toward yourself or others in an attempt to help you move forward.

CARE-SELF AND OTHER: Taking an active role to protect your well-being, health, and happiness — or that of others — particularly in times of stress.

EMPATHY: Understanding what others are thinking or feeling. Holding emotional space for another and in turn feeling for their experience, as in the phrase "walking in someone else's shoes."

RESPECT: Valuing the opinions, experiences, and qualities of others and yourself. Showing dignity and honor to yourself and others.

TRUST: Feeling safe and assured with others or in your environment. A belief in the reliability, ability, or strength of somebody or something.

GENEROSITY: Freely giving or sharing without expectations or agenda. To give yourself or your resources.

BEGINNER'S MIND: Being open to an experience without preconceived notions. To look at and do things with a freshness, as if it were the first time.

HEARTFULNESS/LOVING-KINDNESS: Sending well wishes and warm regards toward yourself, others, and/or the world.

WEEK 1: • Acceptance • Curiosity • Compassion • Nonstriving • • Authenticity • Not Knowing • Being versus Doing • • Gratitude • Presence • Letting Go • Openness • • Nonharmful Judging • Gentleness • Care-Self and Other • Empathy • Respect • • Patience • Forgiveness • Care-Self and Other • Empathy • Respect • • Trust • Generosity • Beginner's Mind • Heartfulness/Loving-kindness

WEEK 2: • Acceptance • Curiosity • Compassion • Nonstriving • • Authenticity • Not Knowing • Being versus Doing • • Gratitude • Presence • Letting Go • Openness • • Nonharmful Judging • Gentleness • Care-Self and Other • Empathy • Respect • • Patience • Forgiveness • Care-Self and Other • Empathy • Respect • • Trust • Generosity • Beginner's Mind • Heartfulness/Loving-kindness •

WEEK 3: • Acceptance • Curiosity • Compassion • Nonstriving • • Authenticity • Not Knowing • Being versus Doing • • Gratitude • Presence • Letting Go • Openness • • Nonharmful Judging • Gentleness • Care-Self and Other • Empathy • Respect • • Patience • Forgiveness • Care-Self and Other • Empathy • Respect • • Trust • Generosity • Beginner's Mind • Heartfulness/Loving-kindness •

WEEK 4: • Acceptance • Curiosity • Compassion • Nonstriving • • Authenticity • Not Knowing • Being versus Doing • • Gratitude • Presence • Letting Go • Openness • • Nonharmful Judging • Gentleness • Care-Self and Other • Empathy • Respect • • Patience • Forgiveness • Care-Self and Other • Empathy • Respect • • Trust • Generosity • Beginner's Mind • Heartfulness/Loving-kindness •

WEEK 5: • Acceptance • Curiosity • Compassion • Nonstriving • • Authenticity • Not Knowing • Being versus Doing • • Gratitude • Presence • Letting Go • Openness • • Nonharmful Judging • Gentleness • Care-Self and Other • Empathy • Respect • • Patience • Forgiveness • Care-Self and Other • Empathy • Respect • • Trust • Generosity • Beginner's Mind • Heartfulness/Loving-kindness •

CHOSEN QUALITY for the WEEK:

_____

CHOSEN QUALITY for the WEEK:

_____

CHOSEN QUALITY for the WEEK:

_____

CHOSEN QUALITY for the WEEK:

_____

CHOSEN QUALITY for the WEEK:

_____

18 : YOUR BASIC NEEDS

*H*uman needs are those needs that, when met, allow you to survive, function, thrive, and to have a general sense of wellness and well-being. What each person needs to feel well and have a general sense of well-being in their life is different. There are two types of human needs—basic and fundamental. This activity focuses on *basic needs*, which are those abilities, goods, or services necessary for a minimum standard of living to survive and function day to day. These basic needs—water, food, shelter, clothing—are often met for people in first world countries since they are often automatic and go without saying. It is when one or more of these needs aren't being met that they get noticed and missed. The point of noticing them and taking active time to consider them is not to feel bad for having your needs met, but rather is a way to remind yourself that you have these needs, abilities, and resources that are provided to you day in and day out. Remembering that your basic needs are being met is a valuable part of taking in the good.

CAN YOU STAY WARM?

Take in the Good: Take Action

The list on the next page shows some of the basic needs of your daily life that are often met for you. Please check off all of the abilities, goods, and services that are meeting your needs right now. Take a few moments after marking each one to recognize what it might be like if you didn't have that ability, good, or service. Take the time to take in the good and consider these needs as part of your resource bank to remind yourself of in hard times. Even when you feel depleted, empty, stressed, and so on, you do have things going right for you even if you don't feel it at that moment. Remembering these can sometimes help you when you are down a rabbit hole and feeling piled on with your to-do list, or on a hamster wheel where thoughts can't seem to stop.

Take in the Good: Takeaway

Acknowledging that these basic needs are being met for you is a reminder that there is more right than there is wrong with you at any one moment.

YOUR BASIC NEEDS

— Can you see?

— Can you hear?

— Can you drink clean water when you are thirsty?

— Can you breathe clean air?

— Can you eat when you are hungry?

— Did you wake up today?

— What luxuries do you have?
— Electricrty
— A roof over your head
— Warm clothes

19 : YOUR FUNDAMENTAL NEEDS

SAFETY, SATISFACTION, AND CONNECTION

The second type of human needs are *fundamental needs*. Psychologist Rick Hanson says that people's fundamental needs are safety, satisfaction, and connection. There are two things to consider: First, you are fundamentally okay right now. Second, at any given moment there is more right with you than wrong with you. Pause for a moment to notice and take in those two statements. Basic needs are often met automatically and without a lot of effort. However, when it comes to fundamental needs, there is more fluctuation and variance in how these needs are met, and so they tend to have more of an impact on your general sense of well-being and your ability to thrive. Look at the following areas of your life—health, freedom, relationships, community, education, and career—much of your time is spent on achieving and maintaining these areas so that you feel safe, satisfied, and connected. When one or more of your fundamental needs aren't being met, your brain is alerted to this and in turn activates you to do something to get your needs met. If you are able to, you will usually do something to get that need met. Your brain wants you to feel safe, satisfied, and connected, not vulnerable, threatened, or rejected.

Take in the Good: Take Action

Part I: Your Fundamental Needs: Safety, Satisfaction, and Connection

The first column of the activity lists your fundamental needs; the next two columns have boxes for you to fill in the types of feelings that either support or discourage the meeting of those needs. The key is to tune in to and make a deliberate effort to engage the people, places, things, events, or situations in your life that support you and allow you to feel that your needs are being met; list those in the *Support* column. Conversely, think of those things that do not support you, but rather cause stress or discourage your needs from being met; list those in the *Discourage* column.

Part II: Your Fundamental Needs Assessment: ARGR

To help you further assess your fundamental needs, read more about ARGR (Attention, Reflection, Gratitude, and Routine) on the second page of this activity. In the *Notes* column:

ATTENTION: Write those needs that are being met the most for you right now and in which areas—health, freedom, relationships, community, education, and career.

REFLECTION: Write down any beneficial or positive thoughts you have and take them in—by noticing and attending to them for thirty seconds to one minute.

GRATITUDE: Write down what you are grateful for. Write what parts of your life are working right. Be grateful for them.

ROUTINE: Write down anything in your daily routine that you have found most helpful to getting your needs met.

Try to do the ARGR review every day so that you can become comfortable doing an assessment of your needs.

Take in the Good: Takeaway

When you are aware of what supports and encourages your fundamental needs for safety, satisfaction, and connection, you can deliberately engage with those people and things that support those needs. You can then consider changing those relationships and things that discourage or keep your needs from getting met.

YOUR FUNDAMENTAL NEEDS: SAFETY, SATISFACTION, AND CONNECTION

FUNDAMENTAL NEED:	FEELINGS THAT ACTIVATE IT:	
	SUPPORT	DISCOURAGE
Safety .and. Peace		• Feeling a pain or threat • Feeling vulnerable
Satisfaction .and. Contentment		• Experiencing something unpleasant • Feeling unhappy, sad, or alone
Connection .and. Love		• Feeling a sense of loss • Feeling rejected by another person

YOUR FUNDAMENTAL NEEDS ASSESSMENT: ARGR

ARGR	NOTES:
ATTENTION: Pay attention to which of your fundamental needs are being met right now: safety, satisfaction, and/or connection.	
REFLECTION: Reflect on and take in feeling safe, satisfied, and/or connected at this moment in time. Keep any of these beneficial thoughts or feelings with you for the rest of the day.	
GRATITUDE: Be grateful for your safety, satisfaction, and/or connection. Acknowledge what parts of your life are working right instead of focusing on what isn't going well.	
ROUTINE: Get into a routine of going through this needs assessment every day. Be grateful when even your most basic needs are being met. By doing so, you start building your gratitude muscles. Feeling grateful can improve your physical and mental health.	

20 : GETTING YOUR NEEDS MET

ARE YOU HALT?

You can notice, attend to, be with, and move through your physical and emotional feelings. Feelings, even painful ones, provide you with direct information about what you need and what actions you might take to get those needs met. Some feelings in particular—hunger, anger, loneliness, and tiredness—are useful to attend to as they are often letting you know your needs aren't being met. Use HALT (Hungry, Angry, Lonely, Tired) to identify what you are feeling and what you are in need of. You are taking care of yourself when you attend to and fulfill any of these needs.

Take in the Good: Take Action

On the next page, read over the items in the first column and ask yourself the questions in each box. If you are currently hungry, angry, lonely, or tired—or more than one of those—use the acronym NAME (Notice, Assess, Make, Engage) right now to get your needs met. If you don't feel hungry, angry, lonely, or tired, pick one you often feel and use it to role-play.

NOTICE: Noticing is the first part to getting a need met. Notice your thoughts, physical sensations, and emotions. Write what you notice next to the *N*.

ASSESS: Assess what might have caused you to be hungry, angry, lonely, or tired. Consider the context, the people, places, things, or situations that are involved. Be a detective. List your findings next to *A*.

MAKE: List what changes you can make to get the need met. For example, if you are hungry you can eat. List what changes you are going to make next to *M*.

ENGAGE: Engage in the needed change you just listed. Next to *E* list how you feel after you engaged in the action to fix the need.

You can come back to this activity whenever you are feeling hungry, angry, lonely, and/or tired and work through it with NAME to get your need(s) met.

Take in the Good: Takeaway

Honor and be present to your needs. Notice when you are Hungry, Angry, Lonely, or Tired (HALT) and eat, connect, and sleep or rest as needed. Remember to go through the process of noticing, assessing, making, and engaging (NAME) anytime you are stuck and need to get one or more of these needs met.

GETTING YOUR NEEDS MET

ARE YOU H.A.L.T.?

		NAME
HUNGRY	Have you eaten recently? **You might need** a **SNACK.**	
ANGRY	Are you angry at some **PERSON, PLACE, THING,** or **SITUATION**? Acknowledge that you're feeling angry; take care of yourself — maybe by taking a break or a personal time-out.	
LONELY	Do you feel **LONELY**? Are you lacking connection with others? Do what you can to engage with another person or group of people.	
TIRED	Have you gotten enough **SLEEP**? If not, take a **NAP** or go to **BED** when you can.	

21 : POSITIVE SELF-CARE ACTIVITIES TO RESOURCE YOURSELF

Your brain gets activated when one—or more—of your fundamental needs aren't being met. It alerts you to do something, to take action to get your needs met. There are a number of things you can do to meet your needs, such as engaging in positive activities to take in the good and taking the time to attend to and notice your pleasant moments. One way to support your fundamental human needs is to make sure you are taking care of yourself—engaging in self-care. You can engage in self-care by doing self-care activities—those positive behaviors and healthy things you enjoy doing that fill you up and nourish you.

When you engage in self-care activities you are filling up your bank of well-being. When your needs are met, you generally feel happy, satisfied, content, peaceful, healthy, and have a general sense of overall wellness. When your needs are not met, you can often feel tired, exhausted, frustrated, ill, unhealthy, drained, or depleted. If you have been engaging in self-care activities on a regular basis, you have been adding coins to your well-being bank so that when things are difficult and you don't have time to attend to and take care of yourself, you aren't at zero. Those self-care coins you have in the bank can at least help you feel slightly less crummy.

Taking in the good is not only about taking care of yourself and feeling good in the moment, it is also about taking in, really noticing, and enjoying those self-care activities you do. In this way, you are adding coins to your bank. Those self-care coins you have stored will help you be better able to tolerate and manage whatever difficulties life throws your way—stressors, disappointments, and the like.

Take in the Good: Take Action

The next page shares some examples of positive self-care activities you can do. Mark all of those activities you enjoy doing or can do. Next, star or highlight your top five. Remember that it is important, if not necessary, to engage in self-care activities regularly.

ENJOY A WALK IN NATURE

Take in the Good: Takeaway

When you engage in self-care you are taking care of yourself right now, and you also get the added benefit of having a resource that you can use later. When difficulties arise, you are better able to tolerate them and deal with them if your well-being bank isn't on empty. Engage in self-care activities to fill you and your well-being bank up.

POSITIVE SELF-CARE ACTIVITIES TO

RESOURCE YOURSELF

- [ ] Get outside and move and/or sweat
  - [ ] Practice mindfulness and relaxation techniques
- [ ] Spend time with an animal, walking your dog or petting your pet, for example
  - [ ] Do something for yourself that you often do as a kind gesture for someone else
- [ ] Say something kind to yourself
  - [ ] Play one of your favorite songs (maybe even dance or sing to it)
- [ ] Take a few deep breaths
  - [ ] Laugh
- [ ] Take a nap
  - [ ] Exercise
- [ ] Practice grounding techniques
  - [ ] Use your grounding focal points (i.e. fingers, hands, breath, heart, and feet.)
- [ ] Write in a journal, doodle, and/or draw
  - [ ] Write a thank-you note to yourself
- [ ] Write down 3-5 things you're grateful for
  - [ ] Call someone who cares about you instead of just sending them a text
- [ ] Watch the sunrise or sunset
  - [ ] Look up at the stars at night
- [ ] Cook a healthy meal, maybe with someone who nourishes and supports you.
  - [ ] Go on a walk, maybe with someone who is supportive in your life
- [ ] Take a short break, mindful pause, or moment
  - [ ] Step away from someone or something that is stressful, painful, or harmful
- [ ] Take a bath or shower
  - [ ] Smell something pleasant (a flower, candle, essential oil, a spice, perfume/cologne)

22 : THE SELF-CARE WATER BOTTLE

One prime way to be for yourself is to engage in self-care. *Self-care* is defined as giving attention to and engaging in ways that support your physical and psychological well-being. When you take care of yourself, you are saying to yourself that you matter. Self-care helps you get your needs met and builds up your well-being bank. Ask yourself and consider these questions:

- Who are the people who are on your side, supporting and encouraging you?
- What places do you go that enhance your mood?
- What material objects make you happy or bring you peace or joy?
- What are things you like to do that improve your overall sense of wellness or well-being?

Take in the Good: Take Action

On the water bottle on the next page, write, draw, color, or mark all the things you can think of that fill you up, nourish, and support you. Include in the outline of the stickers all the things you can that fill up your self-care water bottle. Here are some examples of what to include on your water bottle if you need some prompts:

- Answers to the questions you just thought about from above
- The things you enjoy doing, from the *Take in the Good* activity
- Self-care activities you marked as liking in the last activity
- The names of people or pets that are important to you
- Logos of your favorite bands, music lyrics, or powerful quotes from people
- Images of your hobbies or interests you have

Take in the Good: Takeaway

You can't pour from an empty water bottle! Engaging in self-care is showing yourself that you matter and is a way for you to be there for yourself and provide yourself with a general sense of well-being. Keep your water bottle full!

THE SELF-CARE WATER BOTTLE

23 : TAKE IN BENEFICIAL EXPERIENCES WITH H.O.T.

LEARN TO RESOURCE YOURSELF

Positive neuroplasticity indicates that by attending to a pleasant or positive activity—taking in the good—even for a short period of a time throughout the day, you increase your mental tilt toward the positive and the likelihood of growing positive neural connections that move away from the automatic tendency toward the negative.

To take in the good, you need to have positive and beneficial experiences. Think about building and keeping a campfire. To get a fire going, you need materials—wood, kindling, and matches. Beneficial experiences are the materials—those positive and pleasant moments in your life, whether big or small, that you can "take in." When a campfire burns bright, it is like when an experience fills you with a sense of happiness, contentment, satisfaction, peace, and well-being. When you notice and attend to the pleasant and positive aspects of your beneficial experiences, this is the process of taking in the good. When you take in the good, you get to enjoy the moment and benefit from it while the experience is taking place. Enjoy your campfire while it is burning.

You can deepen your campfire experience by adding extra wood to it to keep it going for longer. Maybe you can make your beneficial experience even better by having s'mores while the fire is going, thereby savoring it and deepening its impact. By attending to and keeping your campfire going you add value to the experience while it is taking place. Another benefit from taking in the good is that you are also resourcing yourself at the same time. If you attend to and savor the beneficial experience, even for a mere thirty seconds, you are creating a lasting resource for your well-being bank. You are creating internal resources you can call on when you are feeling emotionally and physically depleted and drained.

There are so many times, day in and day out, that pleasant moments arise, and these beneficial experiences go unused because you barely notice them before you move past them. You can extend the value that pleasant moments and beneficial experiences can have when you use HOT.

You can use the advice in the acronym HOT (Have the beneficial experience; Open to the beneficial experience; and Take in the beneficial experience) to help you to resource yourself and fill up your well-being bank!

Take in the Good: Take Action

Look at the scenes and read the headings of each box on the left side of the next page. Answer the corresponding questions on the right side.

For the *H*, notice the image of the supplies that will be used to be able to start the campfire and have s'mores.

H : Have the beneficial experience. Notice the beneficial experience you are having, or go and create one.

For the *O*, notice the image of the fire; the beneficial experience is the campfire that is burning.

O : Open to the beneficial experience. Be open to all you can be during the experience. Stay with it while it is taking place. Let the experience become more intense. Open to it in your body. Connect how your body feels to your thoughts and feelings. Be present with your senses and to your thoughts and feelings during the experience.

Lastly, for the *T*, notice the image of the burning campfire; it is glowing brighter than before and is enhanced by the s'mores.

T : Take in the beneficial experience. Let the experience sink into you like water is absorbed into a sponge. Let the experience become part of you. Let the experience become a lasting resource in your well-being bank.

Take in the Good: Takeaway

Practicing HOT (Having the beneficial experience; Opening to the beneficial experience; and Taking in the beneficial experience) is a way to actively engage in your well-being and resource yourself. Take the time to practice HOT whenever you notice you are having a beneficial experience. Doing so creates internal resources you can call on when you are feeling emotionally and physically depleted and drained.

24 : THE PLAYLISTS OF YOUR LIFE

Happy Jams and Depressing Dives

Songs can provide you with powerful experiences. They can evoke emotions and trigger memories—both pleasant and unpleasant. Think of a person who has just been dumped and hears what used to be their favorite song and gets depressed. Think of another person who has just gotten into the college they were hoping for and plays their favorite song and jams, sings, and dances around to it. In each example, the song is going to have a vastly different effect on the person.

The playlists you create and listen to will affect your mood, thoughts, energy level, and memories. Consider the playlists you have right now and think about them in general. Now ask yourself, do you have a *Happy Jams* playlist of songs that support your mood and make you feel good? Do you have a *Depressing Dives* playlist of songs you listen to when you are sad or angry and that tend to keep you down in the dumps? It's like that phrase "turn your frown upside down." You have the power to stay in a frown or change it to a smile. You can create new playlists and attend more to your happy and positive jams than those that might feed negative feelings like feeling depressed. Asking yourself why you are listening to a particular song or set of songs can be valuable. You can use the acronym HOT (Have the beneficial experience; Open to the beneficial experience; and Take in the beneficial experience) to enhance your well-being and to resource yourself with the music you choose to play.

TAKE IN THE GOOD: TAKE ACTION

On the *Happy Jams* playlist, at the top of the next page, write the names of five songs you love that support and nourish your mood. Read the instructions for *H* and list one of the happy jams you are going to listen to. Read *O* and *T* and listen to a favorite song while opening to and taking in the beneficial experience of listening to your happy jam. While focusing on your happy jam, consider what about the song is positive and pleasant and what makes it stick to you like Velcro. Now answer the questions in the spaces provided for *O* and *T*.

On the *Depressing Dives* playlist, at the top of the page, write down the names of five songs that you tend to listen to when you are lonely, discouraged, angry, or depressed. Now pick one of your depressing dive songs, read the instruction for *H,* and choose one of your depressing dives to listen to. Read *O* and *T,* then listen to the song and answer the questions in the spaces provided. While focusing on your depressing dive song, think about being like Teflon and letting the negative effects the song evokes slide off of you.

Notice the differences in your mood and experience while listening to your happy jam and depressing dive.

TAKE IN THE GOOD: TAKEAWAY

Psychologist Rick Hanson writes, "We are Velcro to the negative and Teflon to the positive." Do the opposite of this statement: be Velcro to the positive and Teflon to the negative. Listen to and play music that supports and enhances your mood. Although you might be drawn to a depressing dive, if it brings you down, change that tune.

THE PLAYLISTS of YOUR LIFE

1. _____ ‹‹ ▶ ››

2. _____ ‹‹ ▶ ››

3. _____ ‹‹ ▶ ››

4. _____ ‹‹ ▶ ››

5. _____ ‹‹ ▶ ››

HAPPY JAMS   PLAY

H. Have the beneficial experience. Pick one of your happy jams.

WHAT SONG DID YOU CHOOSE?

WHAT WAS YOUR EXPERIENCE LISTENING TO AND OPENING UP TO YOUR HAPPY JAM?

O. While listening to this song, open to and notice your senses, thoughts, and feelings.

WHAT WAS IT LIKE TO TAKE IN AND SAVOR THE SWEETNESS OF THE NOURISHING AND SUPPORTIVE SONG?

T. Take in your happy jam. Be Velcro and let the song stick to you.

THE **PLAYLISTS** of YOUR **LIFE**

1. _____ «▶»

2. _____ «▶»

3. _____ «▶»

4. _____ «▶»

5. _____ «▶»

DEPRESSING DIVES (PLAY)

H. Have the beneficial experience. Pick one of your depressing dives.

WHAT SONG DID YOU CHOOSE?

WHAT WAS YOUR EXPERIENCE LISTENING TO AND OPENING UP TO YOUR DEPRESSING DIVE?

O. While listening to this song, open to and notice your senses, thoughts, and feelings.

WHAT WAS IT LIKE TO BE TEFLON TO A SONG YOU KNOW IS DRAINING AND DEPLETING TO YOU?

T. Take notice of your depressing dive. Be Teflon and let the song slide off of you.

25 : 130 POSITIVE COPING SKILLS

Another way to provide for your well-being is to utilize *positive coping skills*—mental reminders, strategies, or actions that can support your mood, ease your stress, and help you manage your problems. These skills help you deal with, manage, and live your life in healthier ways.

Take in the Good: Take Action

The following two pages include 130 positive coping skills, mental phrases, tips, or action items you can do to facilitate managing your life and enhancing your well-being. Circle, underline, highlight, or mark in some way all of the skills that you like, that resonate with you, or that you would use. Finally, star or highlight your top ten and list them on the last page of this activity.

Take in the Good: Takeaway

Use positive coping skills to manage your life and enhance your well-being. Doing these can also help you kick stress to the curb.

130 POSITIVE COPING SKILLS

1. Take in the good   2. Listen to and trust your gut   3. Drop in to this moment   4. Notice your five senses   5. Use your grounding focal points   6. Capture your pleasant life moments   7. Resource yourself with HOT   8. Notice your basic needs   9. Get your fundamental needs met   10. Keep yourself safe, satisfied, and connected   11. Assess if you are HALT   12. Ride the waves   13. Manage your stress waves   14. Drop anchor   15. Listen to your wants and needs   16. Ask for what you want and need   17. Get your wants and needs met   18. Engage in self-care   19. Replace self-harm with self-care   20. Self-care isn't being selfish   21. Engage in self-compassion   22. Talk to yourself as you would your best friend   23. Care for your body as it is the only one you have   24. Nurture yourself as you would a pet   25. Your body, mind, well-being, and health are first   26. Surf the urges and fight triggers   27. Take ownership   28. Take responsibility   29. Set and meet deadlines   30. Be with and tolerate thoughts   31. Be with and tolerate feelings and emotions   32. Be in the now, the present, this moment   33. Love yourself   34. Trust the process   35. Don't get stuck in your stories   36. Take action   37. When in self-doubt, fake it till you make it   38. Create new stories   39. Play your happy jams   40. Create a new playlist   41. Don't stay stuck in the problem   42. Get into the solution   43. Be Velcro to the positive   44. Be Teflon to the negative   45. Don't believe everything you think   46. Turn off the to-do list   47. Structure your daily schedule   48. Replace worrying with caring and planning   49. Notice what you can and can't control   50. Don't get prickly   51. Take space from tech devices   52. STOP before you act on a thought or feeling   53. Take mindful downtime   54. Pain is inevitable   55. Perservere through adversity or difficult times   56. Listen to your gut   57. Easy does it   58. Little by slow   59. First things first   60. Be humble   61. Be honest   62. Be loyal   63. Be resilient   64. Be authentic   65. Halt your FEAR (false evidence appearing real)

130 POSITIVE COPING SKILLS

66. Take a mindful pause   67. Create a mindful bubble   68. Try being hopeful instead of being hopeless   69. Try doing something instead of doing nothing   70. Break things down into manageable pieces, steps, or parts   71. Make and follow an action plan   72. When needed, seek out and get professional help   73. Ask someone who is trustworthy for support or help   74. Hang out with your peeps or posse   75. Consider pros and cons   76. Consider the emotional cost   77. Protect yourself   78. Notice the source of the advice   79. Examine the proof   80. Learn from your past mistakes   81. Don't beat yourself up   82. No one will value you more than you value yourself   83. Get yourself out of a bad or harmful situation   84. Notice repeating patterns that are destructive   85. Stop engaging in patterns that are destructive   86. Say what you really think and feel   87. Be assertive   88. Use Mi-Messages to share how you feel   89. Think about what options you have   90. Play out the end of the movie   91. Plant seeds and pull weeds   92. Plan it out   93. Make the best of the situation you are in   94. Set boundaries when needed   95. Be creative   96. Be imaginative   97. Inspire yourself   98. Follow something that motivates you   99. Consider your choices   100. Acknowledge and remind yourself of your strengths, talents, and gifts   101. Celebrate being perfectly imperfect   102. Pat yourself on the back   103. Take breaks if you are working too long   104. Practice mindfulness   105. Be in an attitude of gratitude   106. Respect yourself and others   107. Ask others for help when needed   108. Pace yourself   109. Say NO when needed   110. Choose safety first   111. Seek understanding and create meaning   112. Accept diversity   113. If one way doesn't work, try another   114. Cry if you are sad and need to cry   115. If you are angry, breathe through it   116. Get out of and end bad relationships   117. Be for yourself   118. Don't hang with haters   119. Hang with people who nourish and support you, not those who drain and deplete you   120. Leave a bad situation   121. You can always choose to do something different   122. No one can take away your feelings   123. Sometimes a pain just wants to be heard   124. Pay attention to physical and mental red flags   125. Put your healing first   126. Protect your own values and opinions   127. Let things go   128. Take a break with the 3 Bs: Body, Breathe, Begin   129. Change perspective: Zoom in and out   130. Rise strong and be a survivor

top ten Positive Coping Skills

1.

2.

3.

4.

5.

6.

7.

8.

9.

10.

26 : PLANT SEEDS AND PULL WEEDS

Knowing what is nourishing and supportive to you as well as those things that are draining and depleting can take some thought and consideration. For example, at first glance people staying up late using social media might appear to be nourishing themselves. But in reality, it is draining because they are missing out on sleep, which then affects their functioning and health the next day when they find they are having a hard time keeping their eyes open. Doing things that nourish and support you and doing less of what drains and depletes you are the aims of this activity. *Planting seeds* helps you to grow positive experiences and provides you with lasting resources for overall well-being. You can plant, cultivate, and grow these positive and beneficial "seeds." You can also *pull weeds* by ridding yourself of the people and things in your life that are a drain or stress on you. Of course, it takes effort, but minimizing as many unneeded weeds as possible will help you cultivate your focus on bringing the good into your life.

Take in the Good: Take Action

Under *In Your Life* on the *Plant Seeds* page, list all the positive things you can think of that nourish and replenish you—consider your friends, family, things you like to do, and so on. Under *Today*, consider from the minute you woke up until right now all the things that have helped you thrive emotionally or physically—eating breakfast, washing your face, putting on a warm sweater, cuddling with your pet, having a good interaction with your friend—whatever it might be that benefited you in some way.

Now under *In Your Life* on the following page titled *Pull Weeds*, list all the negative things you can think of that drain and deplete you—consider people you have a conflict with, things you don't like or could potentially harm you in some way, and so on. Under *Today*, consider from the minute you woke up until right now all the things that have in some way hindered your taking in the good and resourcing your-self and those that haven't supported your well-being—a fight with a friend, tripping when you were walking and texting at the same time, focusing on the bad grade on your test, or that negative thing someone posted about you—whatever it might be that harmed you in some way.

Writing these things down provides you with a lot of useful infor-mation. It gives you a very clear picture of that which nourishes and supports you as well as those things that drain and deplete you. This then puts you in the driver's seat when it comes to where you choose to put your focus and attention.

Take in the Good: Takeaway

Focus on planting seeds and pulling weeds to facilitate your growth, development, and well-being. Spend time with those people and on doing the activities that nourish and fill you up and spend less time and energy on those that drain and deplete you.

Planting seeds!

Pulling Weeds!

Plant Seeds

That which Nourishes and Supports you

TODAY:

IN YOUR LIFE:

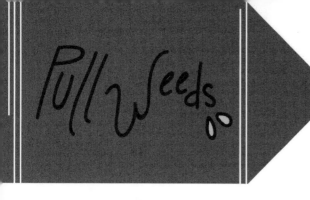

Pull Weeds

That which Drains and Depletes you

TODAY:

IN YOUR LIFE:

27 : FEELING YOUR FEELINGS

The human body provides you with constant information about how you are feeling, what you are thinking, and if you are in physical pain. This information serves to help you function and provide for your health and well-being. What you do with this information affects the decisions you make and the actions you take. It is extremely useful and important to know just how you are feeling. Your body tends to provide you with more accurate information than your mind. Therefore, attending to feelings and the physical cues your body provides can help you tune in and identify how you actually are from one moment to the next. Knowing how you actually feel can be challenging because people often turn to their thoughts rather than their feelings. For example, someone might say "I think I feel," which is actually a thought, not a feeling. Or someone might have more than one feeling at the same time, which can be confusing to them.

You have the power to affect your mood. Try this: Right now, smile even if you don't have something to smile about. Notice how your mood changes. Now make a funny face. Notice how your mood shifts yet again.

Take in the Good: Take Action

You will see an expansive range of feelings on the next page. The feelings in the two columns on the left are often considered unpleasant compared to those in the two columns on the right. Go through and check all those feeling words you identify with. In the blanks, write down feelings that are not listed that you experience. Now under *My Top 5*, list those feelings you have most often.

Turn your frown upside down! If your feelings tend to lean more toward the unpleasant, think of the skills you have and are learning in this book that you could apply and would help tilt you more to pleasant feelings and less toward those that are unpleasant. Even when you are in pain or are hurting, use your list as information—pain is there for a reason.

Take in the Good: Takeaway

Give yourself permission to feel your feelings. You have the power every moment to change your mood, engage in activities, and spend time with people in order to shift that frown upside down.

Feeling Your Feelings

PLEASANT

FEELINGS VOCABULARY:

Afraid	Angry	Happy	Calm
Frightened	Enraged	Joyful	Safe
Scared	Prickly	Glad	Satisfied
Worried	Moody	Thrilled	Content
Jealous	Pity	Surprised	Loving
Envious	Out of Sorts	Excited	Grateful
Hopeless	Scared	Fantastic	Playful
Distressed	Furious	Delighted	Chill
Stressed	Resentful	Anticipatory	Peaceful
Helpless	Irritated	Confident	Worthwhile
Hurt	Ashamed	Ecstatic	Trusting
Worthless	Disgusted	Optimistic	Creative
Guilty	Nasty	Secure	Kind
Depressed	Yucky	Hopeful	Healthy
Distraught	Sorrowful	Free	Connected
Miserable	Grief-stricken	Purposeful	Enthusiastic
Sad	_____	_____	_____

— MY TOP 5 —

_____

_____

_____

_____

_____

UNPLEASANT

28 : DON'T GET PRICKLY

Know How You're Feeling

When a puffer fish gets nervous and feels it is being attacked or threatened in some way it inflates itself as a protection. The puffer fish has a feeling and expresses it by puffing out, an automatic physical response. However, human beings might not be sure what they're feeling; maybe—like a puffer fish—there is this automatic physical response without the direct awareness of connecting it to a feeling. Sometimes people have a felt sense that can't be put into words. There are many feelings, such as prickly, puffy, edgy, odd, strange, and so on, that aren't typically in one's "feelings vocabulary" but nonetheless might be the way someone is feeling. As a puffer fish, people are able to experience their feelings physically, with physical symptoms. It is also possible that people experience their feelings emotionally. The point being that feelings can be experienced and expressed a number of different ways.

Think about any feelings you have and identify with but that don't necessarily fit in the traditional categories. Maybe you have a felt sense about them or experience feelings physically as with a headache or shallow breathing or feeling prickly. It is useful to expand your awareness of how you experience your feelings because this can provide you with information about how you are doing—if you are safe, satisfied, connected, stressed, and the like. If you are feeling an unpleasant feeling, is there something you can do about it? What, if anything, are you able to change in your environment so that you can get to a more neutral, calm, peaceful, or pleasant state?

TAKE IN THE GOOD: TAKE ACTION

Look at the saguaro cactuses on the next page and notice the different feelings listed on the bottom: *calm, sad, angry, happy*.

1. Think about the different people in your life and think about what feelings they most often elicit in you. List their names in the corresponding cactuses for how you most feel when you are around them.
2. Think about some of the interactions you have had in the last two weeks with those closest to you. When thinking of those interactions, notice how you tended to feel overall. You can write any of the specific instances, situations, and events you want in the appropriate feeling cactus.
3. Now think about the places you tend to go and write on the appropriate cactus how you tend to feel when you go to each particular place—examples include a sporting event, the mall, a coffee shop, and so on.
4. Think about some of the objects or material things in your possession that you have the most contact with and think about how they would be placed on the different cactuses. Some objects you might consider include your phone, computer, keys, coffee cup, jacket, water bottle, jewelry, and so on.

Which feeling cactus has the most writing in it? Do you tend to feel calm and happy or sad and angry? Take this as information and let it guide you moving forward.

TAKE IN THE GOOD: TAKEAWAY

When feeling prickly, puffy, edgy, odd, or like a puffer fish do things to take in the good and resource yourself. Every moment you can change how you feel. No one can take away your feelings, and feelings, like waves, will pass!

USING MI-MESSAGES

You positively assert yourself when you state, express, defend, maintain, or put into words your feelings, needs, wants, and beliefs while being mindful, honest, and respectful. One way to assert yourself is to tell someone how you feel. When you tell someone how you feel, no one can tell you that isn't how you feel because it is your feeling. A *Mi-Message* is a mindful I-Message. The *I-Message,* a term first coined by psychologist Thomas Gordon, is a communication asserting one's feelings, beliefs, and values. By staying mindful when creating and implementing your I-Message, it can evolve into a Mi-Message. You can use a Mi-Message to tell someone how you feel. There are two parts to a Mi-Message.

Part I: Mindful Check-In
Check in with your highs and lows for the day. Assess how you feel physically and emotionally. Notice what thoughts and feelings are present. Let your check-in guide you to whether you go on. If you are in what you consider to be good place, continue on to part II. If you are in a funk, a bad mood, or in a not-so-good place, consider pausing your Mi-Message and returning to it when you are feeling better. You want to write Mi-Messages when you are in a good mind-set and when it comes from your heart.

Take in the Good: Take Action

Part II: Assert Yourself Using Mi-Messages

Read the formula for writing a Mi-Message on the next page. Using real situations and scenarios, complete the two Mi-Messages on the following page to share your feelings with someone. You can choose to give your Mi-Message to the person or not—that is up to you. Giving the message to the person isn't required. If you want to give the message to the person, you should consider if it is safe for you to do so. If it is safe, give the person the note you completed or tell them the Mi-Message verbally.

Take in the Good: Takeaway

One way to assert yourself is to tell someone how their actions or behavior affected you. Using a Mi-Message allows you to share your feelings with another. No one can take away your feelings because they are *your* feelings.

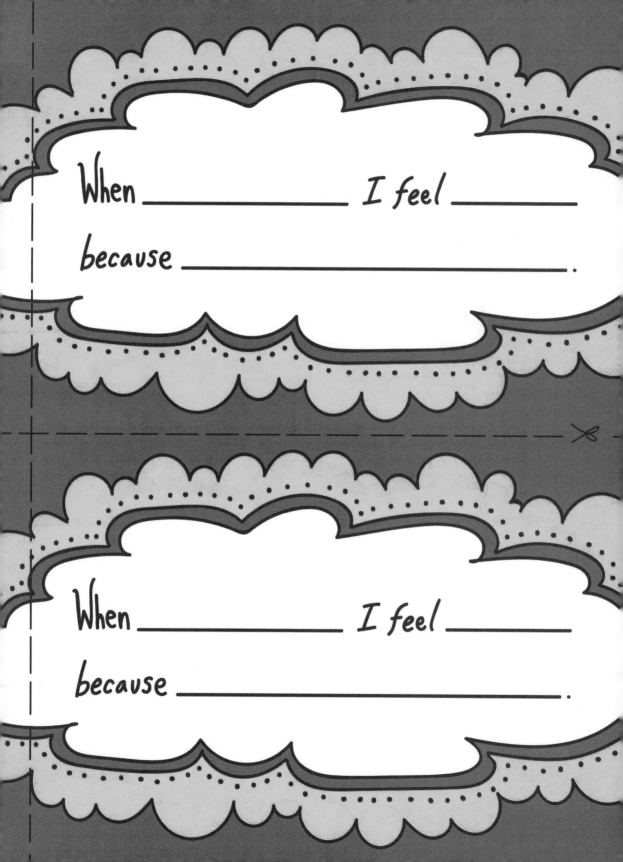

When _____ I feel _____

because _____.

When _____ I feel _____

because _____.

30 : SITTING BODY-SCAN MINDFULNESS PRACTICE

When you are caught up with the hustle and bustle of daily living it is important to take time for yourself and engage in mindfulness practice. Strengthening your mindfulness muscles takes practice and time. When you are stressed or busy, you might feel that those are the times you least want to practice, but in reality those may be the most important times for practice. Mindful practice itself is a type of self-care activity. A practice such as the one described here is also about becoming more aware of your thoughts and feelings because you are quieting the distractions around you that sometimes keep your thoughts and feelings at bay.

The sitting body scan takes you on a tour through your body from the tips of your toes to the top of your head. The main focus is to be aware of your mind and body. Like your body, your mind provides you with useful information if you tune in and pay attention to it. It is important to frequently take a break and check in with your body and mind—your thoughts and feelings.

Below are a few examples of the possible benefits that can come from doing the sitting body scan:

- Offer you information about how you are doing
- Help you to check in with yourself, refuel, and recharge
- Provide you with a short break
- Relax, calm, or center you
- Inform you of your energy level
- Offer you information you hadn't noticed before

Take in the Good: Take Action

As in the "Tips" section of the *Dropping-In Mindfulness Practice* activity, remember to:

- Minimize as many distractions as possible
- Get comfortable
- Read the practice before you do the practice
- Engage in the practice

Read the practice instructions on the next pages, set a timer for six to ten minutes, and do the sitting body-scan practice.

When you are finished, complete the *Mindfulness Practice Debrief* on the last page of this activity.

Take in the Good: Takeaway

Don't forget that practicing mindfulness is engaging in self-care.

Sitting Body-Scan Mindfulness Practice

BEGIN YOUR PRACTICE: LOWER BODY

Bring your attention to both of your feet: your toes, the tops and bottoms of your feet, the balls of your feet, and your heels. If you are wearing shoes, feel the connection of your feet to them.

Proceed to your ankles, noticing the connection between your feet and your lower legs. Attend to your calf muscles and shinbones. Then move up to your knees as they connect to your upper thighs. Notice both hamstring and quadriceps muscles.

Move up to your hips, and notice both feet and legs in their entirety. Be aware of what you recognize along the way. You don't have to flex your muscles or change what is. Just monitor what is present.

Pay attention to the support that both feet and legs provide you.

CONTINUE YOUR PRACTICE: UPPER BODY

Now move up to your stomach and chest. Notice your stomach and lungs expand and release as you breathe.

Reminder: You do not need to breathe in any way; simply notice your body just as it is. You may find that your breath does change; this is normal. Over time, your breathing will shift as you gain experience with this practice.

Move your attention from your chest up to your collarbones and shoulders.

Now bring your attention all the way down your arms to the tips of your fingers on both hands. Witness the air that surrounds your fingers and what the air feels like on the tops and on the fleshy parts of your hands.

Move from your hands to your wrists and up to your forearms, elbows, and upper arms, noticing both biceps and triceps. Recognize what is present along the way and the support that your hands and arms provide you.

As you reach your shoulders, bring your attention down to your lower back, and notice what your lower back is in contact with. Notice your spine and the spaces between your vertebrae as you move up your back to your neck and shoulders.

Let go of any tension or tightness you might be holding in your shoulders. Release any muscles that are engaged here. Let your shoulders, arms, and hands go loose if you can.

Move up from the back of the head to the front of your face. Release any facial expression you might have. If your jaw is clenched, release it. Notice your ears and the soundscape of the sounds in the room.

Notice all the parts of your face. Now bring attention from your face down to your throat, and then to your heart. Try to feel your heart beating. Notice your heart space. If it helps, place one or both hands on your heart.

Now take in all you notice in your entire body. Breathe in fresh air and calmness on the next in-breath, and release any tension in any area of the body you would like on your next out-breath.

PRACTICE CLOSE:

Know that you can take a piece of how you feel to the rest of your day if you so choose. Begin to wiggle your fingers or toes.

If your eyes are closed, gently open them and allow the light to enter. You have now completed the sitting body-scan mindfulness practice.

MINDFULNESS PRACTICE DEBRIEF

ANY **BARRIERS** or **OBSTACLES** YOU WANT TO WORK TO PREVENT OR DECREASE NEXT TIME?

EXAMPLES:

> Quieting distractions
> Knowing your breath changes when you notice it

WHAT DID YOU NOTICE IN YOUR **MIND**: YOUR **THOUGHTS** AND **FEELINGS**?

WHAT DID YOU NOTICE IN YOUR **BODY**? HOW DID YOU TURN TO OR USE YOUR **BREATH**?

ANY **INSIGHTS** YOU WANT TO TAKE AWAY FROM YOUR PRACTICE? ANY **AHA** MOMENTS?

THE RAILROAD PRACTICE

When you are thinking about what happened or what is going to happen, you are missing out on your life as it is unfolding in the now. You aren't actually paying attention to or enjoying what it is you are doing. It is normal and natural to think about the past and future, but such thoughts are often immersed in judging what you did or worrying about what is going to happen. It is useful to see where your mind goes when in thought. In mindfulness practices—like the sitting body scan or drop-in, thoughts will often be noticed more because you are quieting the other distractions that often drown out some of your thoughts. Similarly, when you are trying to sleep at night you might notice thoughts more because it is quiet and that is when thoughts are often brought to the forefront. Instead of getting caught up in a train of thoughts, you can take charge of your thoughts by noticing and witnessing them, but then letting them pass by like the cars of a train.

Take in the Good: Take Action

Read the *Railroad Activity Practice Instructions* on the next page, then set your timer for three to five minutes. This practice focuses on you being a witness to your thoughts passing by like the cars of a train. Notice when you jump on the train. Start your timer, do this practice, and then return here.

Next, on the *Train of Thoughts* page, use the spaces in the train tracks to write down the thoughts that came up for you, particularly those thoughts that were about worries, judgments, and the like. Use this space to leave these thoughts on the paper. You don't have to hold on to them anymore once they are written down. Over time, by writing them down in this way, your thoughts will hopefully shift away from worries and judgments to more nourishing and supportive thoughts. Hopefully, over time, they will become less powerful and take up less brain time.

Take in the Good: Takeaway

Remember that during any mindfulness practice or when your thoughts just won't seem to turn off, you don't need to jump on your train of thoughts. Observe and witness your thoughts as they arise—without clinging or adding to them or trying to ignore or push them away.

RAILROAD ACTIVITY PRACTICE INSTRUCTIONS

Seated in a comfortable position, imagine yourself sitting on top of a hill.

Once you have this image in your mind, look down at the bottom of the hill and see a train track. Picture a train starting to pass.

As you see each car go by, think of each as one of your thoughts.

Without jumping on the train, notice the cars - your thoughts - as they pass.

If you find that one thought keeps popping back up, just notice it.

You can say, *Oh, interesting. This is what I'm thinking right now* and return to noticing your train as it is passing by.

32 : DON'T BELIEVE EVERYTHING YOU THINK

Don't Get Inked

Just because you have a thought, you don't have to believe it. It is useful to ask yourself when you notice a thought, is it true, real, or factual? Worries are a type of thought that people often think are productive—they aren't! Worries will not change the outcome of how something will turn out or change how something went. People can get consumed by worries, by thinking about this or that.

Look at this cephalopod, or squid. When it gets nervous, bothered, or bugged it lets out an ink indicating it is worried. Worries are like a bully: they want attention and typically will not go away until they are noticed. The more you attach to a worry, the more it tends to stick around. Therefore, when you know what you are worried about, you can kick the worries to the curb by noticing them and taking action.

Take in the Good: Take Action

On the lines above the squids on the next page, write down five worries you currently have or tend to have. Now, inside of the squids, list what actions you can take to kick that particular worry to the curb. If you can't think of action items, consider what things you can do to fight back your worry bully and prevent your "inking." You can also fight the worry by doing those things that provide you with a general sense of well-being. Reflect back on any of the things you have learned—things you like to do, any self-care activities, these can help quiet the worries. You are more powerful than you think. Remember, just because you think it, you don't have to believe it or give it more power and attention if you don't want to.

Take in the Good: Takeaway

You can care about the outcome of something, take steps, and follow a plan to affect the worry—instead of worrying. When you are in the now, you aren't worrying about what happened or what is going to happen. You are doing something that creates change.

33 : YOUR GUEST HOUSE

In Rumi's poem "The Guest House" he writes, "This being human is a guest house." Think of yourself as having a metaphorical house in your mind, one that stores your guests—your feelings, thoughts, stories, memories, strengths, weaknesses, cobwebs, and so on. Your mental house holds all your experiences—the good, the bad, the ugly. The thing people often forget about these metaphorical houseguests that come to your house is that they can leave. You can ask them to leave. Similarly, you can say goodbye to those things that have a mental hold on you and are taking up more space than you would like in your house. It isn't to say that an event, conversation, interaction, or moment didn't happen; rather, it is to say okay, this or that happened, but it doesn't have to stay or linger. You can clean your house.

Rumi goes on to say, "Be grateful for whoever comes, / because each has been sent / as a guide from beyond." Know that even in difficult, unpleasant, or painful moments there is most often something that can be gleaned and learned from them. These moments might be opening you up "for some new delight." Sometimes even the worst experience can provide you with useful information. Jon Kabat-Zinn, the founder of the Mindfulness-Based Stress Reduction program for adults, wrote, "Every moment is precious even if in pain." Pains—physical and emotional—are part and parcel of the human condition. It is what you do with your pains and how you move through them that can make all the difference.

Take in the Good: Take Action

On the next page of this activity, list on the front of the house all the welcomed guests—feelings, thoughts, stories, strengths, memories, and so forth—that come to mind. You can include any people, places, objects, or events that you can think of that give your house structure and foundation.

On the following two pages, list all the unwelcomed guests—the cobwebs, stories, pains, traumas, things that hurt when you think of them. Now that you have written these things down, imagine cleaning house and letting these cobwebs go. Letting go doesn't imply forgiveness, you are doing a virtual cleaning. How do you feel now that you have cleaned house?

Take in the Good: Takeaway

Just as it is important to clean your actual house where you live, it is also useful and necessary to clean your mental house. It is useful to get in the habit of knowing what is in your house and what needs to be cleaned to make room for new experiences and guests.

34 : TAKE A MINDFUL PAUSE

Create a Mindful Bubble

Taking a *mindful pause* is a way to take space or the time to check in and provide yourself with a short break. This pause can be from a few seconds to a few minutes or even hours depending on what you need and what is feasible. Sometimes you can't take as long of a pause as you would like—do what you can. In taking this space you are creating a mature time-out, knowing you need to take time and then doing so. It is particularly helpful to take a pause when you are trying to make a decision or having a difficulty or conflict. Creating this time and space can provide for a thoughtful response rather than an impulsive reaction.

Take in the Good: Take Action

Imagine a difficulty or conflict you are having. If you aren't having one right now think of the last one you can remember. Create a mindful bubble around yourself. Look at the image on the next page and see there is a bubble, a space between the person and the others causing this person distress. The *mindful bubble* can provide you with this imaginary space so that you don't have to receive what is coming at you, and you don't have to respond to it if you don't want to. This bubble provides a space between you and a person or people, but this even works with other things or objects and in specific places. Imagine having this remote control: you get to pull it out, hit the *enact mindful bubble* button, and place this bubble around you when needed to give you this imaginary space from what you need space from. When you are taking a mindful pause and it isn't enough, you can engage your imaginary mindful bubble to create the space you might not be getting.

Now, on the following page, work through a difficulty or conflict you are having using the fours Rs (Recognize, Reset, Resource yourself, and Respond). Respond to the inquiries in the spaces below each.

Take in the Good: Takeaway

Taking a mindful pause puts a space between you and a stimulus, allowing for a response. When you are having a difficulty or conflict use the four Rs—recognize the difficulty or conflict, reset, resource yourself, and respond if needed.

MANAGE DIFFICULTIES and CONFLICTS
WITH the FOUR Rs

① RECOGNIZE: Identify the difficulty or conflict. This is a huge first step as it can be hard sometimes to even recognize you are having a difficult time or are in a conflict.
What is the difficulty or conflict you are having? If a person, or people, are involved, include it here.

② RESET: Before letting your thoughts or emotions take over, hit your reset button. Take a mindful pause or create a mindful bubble and write about what you did here. What are you thinking? How are you feeling now?

③ RESOURCE YOURSELF: Assess your fundamental needs for safety, satisfaction, and connection. Consider if these are being activated and need supportive resourcing.
Which of your needs are or aren't being met? Write about it here. What ways, if any, can you take in the good?

④ RESPOND: If action is needed, take some. You can (1) do nothing; (2) change your behavior; or (3) ask another person to change their behavior.
How are you going to respond and proceed?

35 : URGE SURFING

SURF THE URGE

U rge surfers are people who tend to be in a reactive and impulsive place versus a responsive and thoughtful one. *Urge surfing* is a phrase referring to people who are engaging in their harmful urges. These urge surfers might be engaging in self-harm—specifically drug or alcohol use, high-risk situations, or conflictual encounters—without thinking them through. Just because you have an urge or impulse to do something doesn't mean you have to do it. You are in the driver's seat of the decisions you make and the actions you take. You can fight your urges by surfing them. *Surfing the urge* is about noticing the urge you have, staying curious about it and surfing over it without engaging in the urge.

Take in the Good: Take Action

On the next page, under *urge triggers*, list the people, places, things, and situations that trigger your urges or have you urge surfing. In the next column, *your urges*, list what actions, behaviors, or things you do when you are in an urge-surfing state.

On the following page, *Surf the Urge*, read about the three steps to surfing the urge in the first column. Use them to help you surf your urges. If and when an urge still persists, consider using the acronym SOBER, in the second column, to help you respond instead of react to your urges. Psychologist G. Alan Marlatt created SOBER to help put a conscious gap between thoughts and feelings, actions and behaviors. Go through the process of SOBER with one of the urges you listed on the previous page to help you surf your urge.

Take in the Good: Takeaway

It is part of the human condition to have the urge at one point or another to engage in doing something that will harm you. You can choose to surf your urges instead of urge surfing by noticing the urge, staying curious about it, and surfing over the urge wave.

Who are the PEOPLE, PLACES, THINGS, and SITUATIONS that have you URGE SURFING?

Actions, behaviors, things you do when you are Urge Surfing...

URGE TRIGGERS

YOUR URGES

SURF ·the· URGE

Take a mindful pause and a STEP BACK. Surf the urge by 1. Noticing the urge, 2. Staying curious about the urge, and 3. Surfing over the urge waves.

SURFING THE URGE

STEP 1: NOTICE WHAT THE URGE FEELS LIKE. Ask yourself, "Is there a feeling or need that I'm trying to meet when I follow that urge? Am I trying to avoid something else (procrastinating, denying, or pushing away a difficult feeling)?"

STEP 2: STAY CURIOUS ABOUT YOUR URGES. Tell yourself, "Hmm, interesting. This is what the urge feels like right now." Ask yourself, is it a physical sensation, a mental impulse, or a way to avoid something else in the present?

STEP 3: SURF OVER THE URGE WAVES. Remember that urge waves will pass. Like ocean waves that ebb and flow, the urges you have will pass. Don't give in to the urge, and it will eventually subside.

SURF THE URGE: USE SOBER

♥ STOP: Stop where you are. Be present and tune in to what is actually taking place in this moment.

♥ OBSERVE: Observe how you are feeling physically and emotionally.

♥ BREATHE: Take a deep breath. Center your attention on your breathing. Notice where you bring air in on your next in-breath, through your nose or mouth, and where you release air on your next out-breath, through your nose or mouth.

♥ EXPAND: Expand your awareness. Consider what will happen if you keep thinking this thought. Consider what will happen if you keep feeling this feeling. Consider what impact the behavior will have if you engage in it.

♥ RESPOND: Make a decision and respond accordingly. Decide to do something other than this behavior. Use any of the resources and tools in this book to do something different.

36 : YOUR MENTAL LOCKER

In every moment, you have the opportunity to feel how you want to feel and think what you want to think. No one can take away how you feel or what you choose to think about. Your mind—both your feelings and thoughts—is yours. However, when you are the one driving your feelings and thoughts to the negative, it can be hard to get out of that negative feedback loop. It is like running in a hamster wheel trying to get somewhere, but you only end up right back where you started. You have the power to change this negative feedback loop. The first step is having the awareness about what you are thinking and feeling that is harmful to you and then to do what you need to change to a more helpful framework. Think about your mind as a locker.

- It can be difficult to find things.
- It can hold a lot of different things.
- It can have old stuff buried in it.
- It can have clean new fresh stuff in it.
- It can get overwhelming and you can get lost looking in it.

You can let a locker get full and messy when you are in a hurry and keep throwing stuff in there that gets piled high. At other times, you can clean out the locker and get rid of old stuff, throw out trash, and use whatever is in there that is of value to you.

Take in the Good: Take Action

For this activity, think about what is in your mental locker right now. It might take some time to get at the layers of stuff in your locker. There might be some things buried in there that you didn't even realize were there. In the locker on the following page, write down what is in your mental locker. You can use any of the following prompts to help you access what is in your locker.

- What are the things you say or think about yourself that would be considered *negative self-talk*?
- What are your perceived weaknesses or areas in which you lack confidence about yourself?
- What harmful judgments (those judgments not based in truth, fact, or reality) do you have about yourself?
- What have people said about you that is negative, harmful, or hurtful?
- What are painful memories or moments in your life that are hard to get over?
- What stories do you have about yourself that are weighing you down?

Take in the Good: Takeaway

When you are aware of the negative thoughts, judgments, and beliefs you hold in your mental locker you can clean them out. You can give your mental locker the time and attention it needs to become a clean locker, a fresh slate, just like how it appears at the beginning of a new school year.

NO HARMFUL JUDGMENTS ALLOWED

You can combat negative thoughts and beliefs taking up space in your mental locker by focusing on the positives, your strengths, and creating a mantra. A mantra is an ancient practice developed by wise spiritualists centuries ago that aids people in manifesting their thoughts into reality. The Sanskrit word *mantra* comes from the root *man-* ("to think," or the "mind") and *tra-* ("tools" or "instruments"). So a *mantra* is literally an "instrument of thought/of the mind." The idea is that you are an agent of change and capable of being the person you desire. You can live your best life if you want to.

Take in the Good: Take Action

There is no right or wrong way to create your mantra. It is a personal self-statement that is based on your individual beliefs and experiences. It is an expression of that which you most desire and value. To develop your mantra, if you can, create a physical space that is calm and free from distractions. You might even play music that is on your chill playlist or have things that are soothing around you—a candle, dimmed lights, and so on. On the door hanger on the next page, complete the blanks for each of the phrases that begin with *I want*.

I want to be—these are three qualities that are important to who you are. They are how you would describe your best self. If it helps, you can reflect back on the mindful qualities. *Example: I want to be happy, humble, and honest.*

I want to have—these are the three things that are most important in your life. You might consider those things that support your fundamental needs for safety, satisfaction, and connection. *Example: I want to have freedom, love, and compassion.*

I want to do—these are three of your goals and dreams about family, career, and/or educational desires. *Example: I want to go to college, have a family, and live a meaningful life.*

Your Mantra: Write your final mantra at the end by filling in the blanks with one choice from each of the three sections. Your mantra can be something that is true now or something you aspire to be or to have in your life. *Example: I am happy, I have love, and a meaningful life.*

Take in the Good: Takeaway

You can remind yourself of your wants and repeat your mantra to focus on the positive, to motivate you, and to counter the brain's automatic tendency to cling to negative thoughts and feelings.

I want to be

_____ _____ _____

I want to have

_____ _____ _____

I want to do

_____ _____ _____

YOUR MANTRA

I am _____, I have

_____, and

_____.

MY MANTRA

_____

_____

38 : THERMOSTAT SET POINT

Balancing Your Mood

You can visualize your mood as a thermostat. When your temperature reaches 120°F, you might be quite angry, frustrated, and other similar *hot* emotions; conversely, when you are at 0°F, you might be depressed, anxious, sad, worried, and other similar *cool* emotions. But your mood thermostat has a *set point*, the level at which your mood stabilizes. Think about the device or system that heats or cools your house. Let's say 70°F is the thermostat set point where your house is the most comfortable. If the temperature goes up to 80°F, the air-conditioning comes on to reduce the heat and get back to the set point; conversely, if it gets to 60°F, the heater will kick on to bring the temperature up to 70°F. Similarly, you can calibrate and adjust your mood to get to your set point. Here are a few things you can do to adjust your hot or cool moods:

- Take in the good, do something you like to do.
- Engage in self-care activities.
- Turn to positive coping skills.

Take in the Good: Take Action

On the next page, the thermostat has different temperature points of reference, with 70°F set as *your balance point*. In your life, which people, places, objects, and events get you up to 120°? Write them down on the lines between 70°F and 120°F. Next, in your life, which people, places, objects, and events get you down to 0°F? Write them on the lines between 70°F and 0°F.

Looking back at what you wrote, consider which of these you can or might consider changing so that you can maintain your thermostat set point.

Take in the Good: Takeaway

Balancing your mood can be difficult, depending on what is occurring in your life, or the feelings you have from one moment to the next. With deliberate effort you can calibrate and recalibrate as needed to get to your thermostat set point.

With of the hustle and bustle of our fast-paced lives, sometimes it can be hard or even feel awkward to have unscheduled time—the time when we don't do a lot or get a lot done. *Mindful downtime* is a way to take the time you need to recharge and refuel. Just as you eat when you are hungry or sleep when you are tired, taking mindful downtime when you are over-worked, stressed, spent, or depleted is crucial and necessary. It is important to have unscheduled and unstructured time so that you can build up your resources again before you are back at school or work.

Take in the Good: Take Action

Knowing what cues and signs you have that your physical and/or emotional gas tank is on empty is useful because you can use this information to make needed changes. On the next page, read the lists of physical symptoms and emotional cues that are red flags indicating you might need a break and some downtime. Now, list your own physical symptoms and emotional cues on the right-hand side. You can use any from the samples provided, but also consider your own.

You can counter an empty tank with those things that fill up your tank, those downtime activities and things you can do to chill out and relax. These are things that don't necessarily require a lot of attention or mental effort. On the second activity page, *Take Mindful Downtime*, read the *examples of downtime activities to fill up your tank*. Now, using some from that list and others that you like to do, create your own list.

Take in the Good: Takeaway

Taking mindful downtime helps to nourish and support you and increases your general well-being. When you notice the physical symptoms and emotional cues, those red flags that your gas tank is running low, make sure you counter that by engaging in a downtime activity that fills your tank back up.

SIGNS that your PHYSICAL and/or EMOTIONAL gas tank is on EMPTY:

▶ PHYSICAL SYMPTOMS:
- Crying
- Muscle tightness or pain
- Shortness of breath or chest pain
- Stomachache or nausea
- Sweating or trembling

▶ EMOTIONAL CUES:
- Irritable, frustrated, sad, and/or angry
- Tired
- Lack of enjoyment in typically enjoyed activities
- Difficulty focusing
- Feeling overwhelmed
- Feeling more emotional than usual
- Snappy or short-tempered with other people

▶ PHYSICAL SYMPTOMS:

▶ EMOTIONAL CUES:

TAKE MINDFUL DOWNTIME

Your downtime activities that FILL UP YOUR TANK

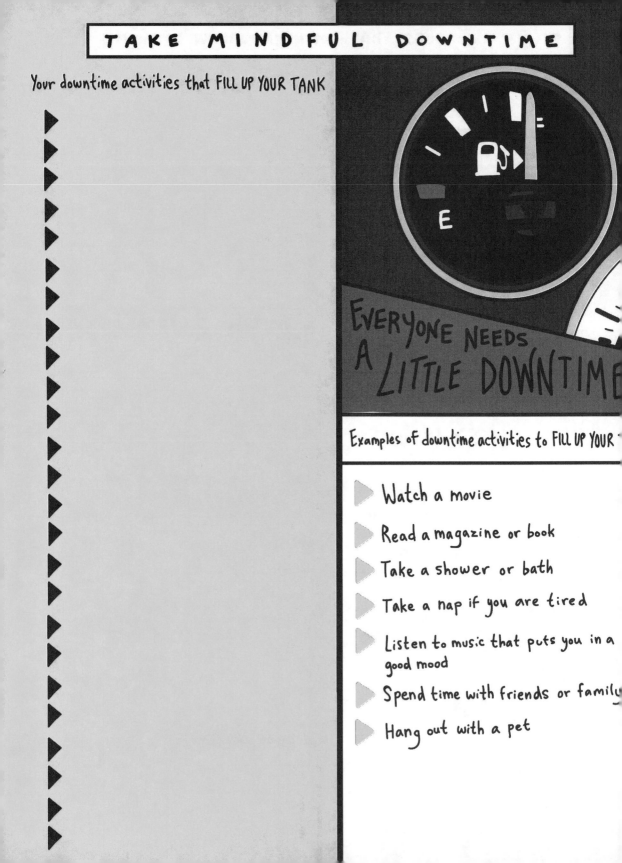

EVERYONE NEEDS A LITTLE DOWNTIME

Examples of downtime activities to FILL UP YOUR

▶ Watch a movie

▶ Read a magazine or book

▶ Take a shower or bath

▶ Take a nap if you are tired

▶ Listen to music that puts you in a good mood

▶ Spend time with friends or family

▶ Hang out with a pet

LEVELS OF SELF-CARE ACTIVITIES

Participating in self-care activities is not only a way for you to take care of yourself, it is making your health and happiness a priority. People often put everyone and everything else in their lives first, even before themselves. However, one of the best things you can do for others is to care for yourself. You can't help others until you are *truly* taking care of yourself. Engaging in self-care activities is essential to staying alive, functioning well, and being healthy. You need to take care of yourself by filling yourself up with healthy things that support, promote, and nourish you every day.

Take in the Good: Take Action

First, consider how much time you spend on self-care. Doing this can help you sort out which self-care activities are more accessible to you.

On the first page of this activity, consider those activities that can take from one to fifteen minutes and write them in the Level I circle. Look on the next page, *Level II*, for examples of activities that range anywhere from around a half hour up to an hour and a half; list your personal Level II activities here. The idea is to do a few Level I activities per day and at least one to three Level II activities per week.

Next, for the *Level III* page, list what activities you do when you say you are *doing nothing* or *taking the day off*. I encourage you to, at least once a month, spend a half to a full day off doing these things. The *Level IV* page asks you to list the people in your life who nourish and support you and whom you can spend at least a half to a full day with, once a month. Each level offers suggestions and possible time intervals. These suggestions are minimums. On the last page, the *Best of Your Self-Care Activities*, list the top activities for Levels I, II, and III and the names of your people for Level IV. Obviously, the more self-care activities you do the better.

Take in the Good: Takeaway

Be there for yourself. Practice bringing self-care activities into your life every day. Engage in Level I, II, and III self-care activities and spend time with healthy people, Level IV.

(Once a month, take a half or full day off.)
• Lie around, nap, sleep
• Garden or spend time in nature
• Wath movies or TV
• Salon or spa visit
• Stay in your pjs or sweats all day
LEVEL III

A MINDFULNESS PRACTICE

When you are in your *head space* you are:

- Thinking of what you just did.
- Thinking of the next thing you need to do.
- Reflecting on your to-do list.
- Worrying, ruminating, judging, or catastrophizing.

You might need to get into your heart space—to what you are feeling. When you are in your head space, you might be missing what your heart space is telling you. It is important to treat yourself and others with kindness and love. When you notice you are thinking and maybe not feeling, you can check in to your heart space.

TAKE IN THE GOOD: TAKE ACTION

Part I: Heart Space Mindfulness Practice

You can get to your heart space by doing the following mindfulness practice.

Step 1: Place one or both hands on your *heart space*—that place on top of your chest, near and encompassing your heart, by your collarbone.

Step 2: Check in with your mood, energy level, sense of safety, satisfaction, and connection.

Step 3: Breathe. You might take one or two deep breaths and notice the breath flow in and out from your nose or mouth, knowing you are bringing cool clean air and oxygen into your body.

Step 4: Wish that all beings (nature, pets, people) and you be filled with happiness, health, love, peace, joy, and truth. May all be filled with these warm wishes and kind regards. May all be filled in their heart space.

Part II: Heart Space Debrief

Go to the *Your Heart Space* page and write or draw in the heart any of the following:

❀ People, places, objects, and events in your life that support and encourage your heart space

❀ Things you do that fill up your heart space

❀ Thoughts or feelings you are having right now after doing this practice

❀ Positive self-statements, quotes you like, words that strike you positively, and so on

Take in the Good: Takeaway

Give yourself permission to turn to your heart space when you notice you are in your head space. Shifting your attention and focus can nourish and support your well-being.

To protect you from harm, your brain is biologically wired to attend to whatever isn't working right, to anything that is bad or negative. This is called the brain's *negative selection bias.* When you pay attention to the parts of your life that are working well and going right—those things that you are grateful for—you compensate for your brain's overemphasis on the negative. You combat your brain's wiring to attend to the negative when you actively attend to the positive. You can do this by focusing on gratitude. *Gratitude* is a way of expressing and experiencing appreciation for what you have in your life—emotionally, physically, spiritually, and so forth. Being grateful is the act of or feeling of gratitude. What parts of your life are you grateful for?

Take in the Good: Take Action

On the gratitude tree on the next page, fill in the leaves with all of the things you are grateful for right now. You might consider what is working well and going right:

- Physically and emotionally
- Socially, with the people in your life that support and fill you up
- Your basic needs—clothes, food, shelter
- Fundamental needs—safety, satisfaction, connection

The things you are grateful for can, but don't have to be, huge themes such as health or family, or they can be the simple things—a cup of tea, a candle, a friend reminding you of something. In times when you feel you are having a miserable time or an awful day it might be hard to feel grateful for much of anything. In these instances, you can *fake it until you make it*. Just consider what is on your person—shoes, clothes, what you are standing or sitting on, that you have this book, that you have a writing instrument.

Take in the Good: Takeaway

There is more right with you than there is wrong at any given moment. You can always shift your mood, even slightly, by thinking of a few things that you are grateful for.

the
gratitude
tree

43 : I SEE YOU AND I HEAR YOU

People often report that their core want and need from other people is to truly be seen and heard—to be listened to without the other person thinking of the next thing they plan to say or thinking about something else entirely. Offering presence to another is a present—*the gift of presence*. Being seen and heard is a two-way street. You can be seen and heard by another person; conversely, you can be there for someone else, letting that person be seen and heard.

Take in the Good: Take Action

The next time you are in a conversation with someone who you feel has listened to you, who has "seen and heard" you, give that person one of the two postcards on the next page.

The next time you see someone in your life who is in a bad way—down in the dumps, sad, having a string of bad luck—give that person one of the postcards to let them know you see them and hear them. If you are available, you might even tell that person that you are there to listen if they want to talk.

Feel free to color and embellish the drawings on the postcards. Perhaps add a sticker, or tape on a wildflower or a sweet treat when you are giving these away. If you are the creative type, engage your creativity and make your own additional I see you and hear you cards.

Take in the Good: Takeaway

Remember, when you are feeling stuck with a problem, or focusing on your own stuff, you can get out of yourself by being there for another. It is a precious gift to offer yourself and others the gift of presence.

44 : LITTLE THANK-YOU NOTES

Acts of Kindness

The Random Acts of Kindness Foundation has scientifically proven that offering thanks and kindness can increase your energy, happiness, life span, pleasure, and serotonin (a type of chemical neurotransmitter in the body that maintains mood and balance). Recognizing that you want to offer thanks, whether to yourself or another, takes some effort on your part, but the power of doing so has a great impact.

You can always express thanks toward yourself. When you engage in self-care, acknowledge the kind acts you have done for yourself. When you do something for another—like being a supportive friend—or when you pat yourself on the back for getting something done, offer yourself thanks. Those are examples of self-gratitude. But you can also express your thanks outwardly by thanking someone for a favor or gesture, a gift or act of generosity, an aspect of their personality, or a specific behavior that has positively affected you in some way.

Take in the Good: Take Action

Look at the *Little Thank-You Notes* on the next page. Writing and offering these little thank-you notes to others is an act of kindness. Engaging in an act of kindness is showing support, compassion, and caring to others.

When it feels right, complete these notes and give them to people. Notice how people respond when you give them out. Notice how you feel when you brighten someone else's day. Lastly, don't forget to thank yourself. Take time to thank yourself for the good job you did on something. Notice how you feel when you acknowledge yourself. It might feel awkward, but remind yourself it is good for your health to be kind to yourself too!

Take in the Good: Takeaway

The positive effects of offering thanks are powerful not only to the receiver but also to you. When you want to increase your mood, give someone a little thank-you note as an act of kindness.

45 : CELEBRATING BEING PERFECTLY IMPERFECT

Culturally, perfection is often strived for and honored, whereas imperfection is often viewed as weak and to be avoided. In the ancient Japanese art technique of Kintsugi, broken pottery is fixed by repairing it with precious gold. Instead of hiding the damage, the gold helps it to stand out, celebrating the object's uniqueness and making it more precious than it was before.

This Kintsugi art technique to fix with gold connects with the Eastern philosophy of *wabi-sabi*, which is finding beauty in the imperfect or damaged, such as with the pot pictured here. This approach to finding beauty among the imperfect can be applied as a life lesson and be seen as an extension of how people see and value themselves—the strengths, talents, and gifts they have. You can't be someone else, because that person is already taken, but you can honor and take in that which makes you *you* and celebrate being perfectly imperfect.

WABI-SABI POT

Take in the Good: Take Action

The phrase *celebrating being perfectly imperfect* was coined by the founders of Connect Be Well, Ana O'Sullivan and Kerri Mahoney. Celebrate who you are and write in the shapes on the next page, listing all of the things you can in the different cues provided in each shape. If you can't come up with answers for some of these prompts, that is fine; perhaps you can talk to and inquire about them with those you trust and that nourish and support you—friends, family, teammates, and so on. In the category *Fun Facts* at the top of the page, list anything unique and cool about what hobbies you like to do, or anything someone wouldn't know about you just by looking at you from the outside.

Take in the Good: Takeaway

People who strive for perfection tend to feel empty and chronically feel like they aren't good enough. People who celebrate their perfections as well as honor and hold with compassion their imperfections are often much more content and enjoy a stronger sense of overall well-being. You are perfectly imperfect just as you are!

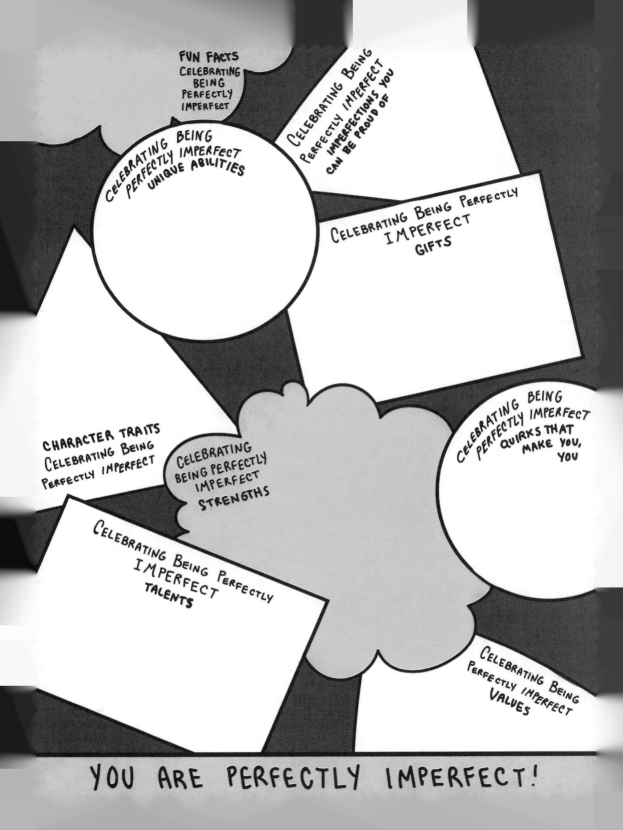

etting go can be explained as the process of releasing, lessening, or removing the weight—physical and emotional—that something has on you. Letting go is the process of taking away the feelings or perceived power a person, place, thing, or event has over you. When you let go, you can bring a sense of freedom and clarity into your life. Letting go is a personal practice; it is done by you and for your benefit only. Letting go does not imply forgiveness or that something didn't occur or happen to you.

Take in the Good: Take Action

Mentally holding on to something takes a lot of energy. On the next page, write whatever is weighing you down or taking up your mental space in the *Let-It-Go Box*. Once you do this you don't have to hold on to those things anymore. They are now being held in this symbolic box. Ideas for what to put in your let-it-go box:

- Negative self-judgments
- Worries or anxieties
- Pains or stressors
- People who you have conflict with
- Memories of things you have done that you are still beating yourself up about
- Anything else you want to free yourself from that may be causing you suffering

If this let-it-go box works for you, consider creating another let-it-go box. Take any box—like a shoebox—and decorate it on the outside. When things come up that you get stuck on or weigh you down consider writing them on slips of paper and putting them in the box. You can then ask that the power these things have over you be removed. You can go back into the box later and read what you put in there and consider (1) if the issue is still affecting you, put it back in or write a new one; (2) if it is resolved, or has shifted or changed, acknowledge that; and (3) when possible, shred or throw out what doesn't need to take up space in your box anymore.

Take in the Good: Takeaway

Letting go is a process that is possible! It takes courage, strength, and willingness to let something go, but doing so can provide much-needed relief. Letting go can help you to live your life more fully and on your own terms.

47 : GROWING YOUR RESOURCES

Growing resources for yourself is like putting a flower bouquet together. As you collect flowers, eventually you'll have enough to make an entire bouquet. It takes deliberate effort to take in the good and grow your resources. You just need to remind yourself to take the time to acknowledge the good, to open to it, and take it in.

Take in the Good: Take Action

On the next page, consider the resources you have or things you can do to resource yourself and grow your flower bouquet. Consider the following as a way to complete your bouquet:

On numbers 1–2, list two people in your life who nourish, support, and fill you up.

On numbers 3–4, list two of your strengths. If you can't think of your strengths, reflect on the ones people have told you that you possess.

On numbers 5–6, list two of the things you are grateful for right now.

On numbers 7–8, list two things that you enjoy doing.

On numbers 9–10, list two positive coping skills that come to mind that you can use when you want or need them.

Take in the Good: Takeaway

Remember to reflect on the resources you already have that make up your flower bouquet. It is important to build on your bouquet and/or make entirely new arrangements to keep you fresh and in an attitude of gratitude.

48 : THE 5 GS

BE IN AN ATTITUDE OF GRATITUDE

When you practice an attitude of gratitude, you are actively taking the time to think about what you are grateful for. One of the best ways for combating your brain's innate difficulty to take in the good is to be in an attitude of gratitude. What are five things you are grateful for in your life today? Reflect on these five things you are thankful to have in your life. If you can't think of five things, come up with what you can. Consider being grateful for your:

- basic needs you have that are being met right now;
- fundamental needs that provide you safety, satisfaction, and connection;
- abilities;
- health;
- family, friends, or pets.

Take in the Good: Take Action

For a week, every day, think of five things you are grateful for and write them down next to the corresponding Gs (1 through 5) on the next sheet. Each time you write one thing down that you are grateful for, notice how you feel. Consider attending to each of these 5 Gs for around thirty seconds each as a way to be a resource for yourself and combat the negative selection bias. Doing this exercise can engage your brain to take in the good and provide your well-being bank with additional resources.

Take in the Good: Takeaway

When wake up, before you go to sleep at night, during the day, or when you are stressed, think of five things you are grateful for. Getting into a routine of considering what you are grateful for will enhance your well-being. Remember to bring an attitude of gratitude to your day.

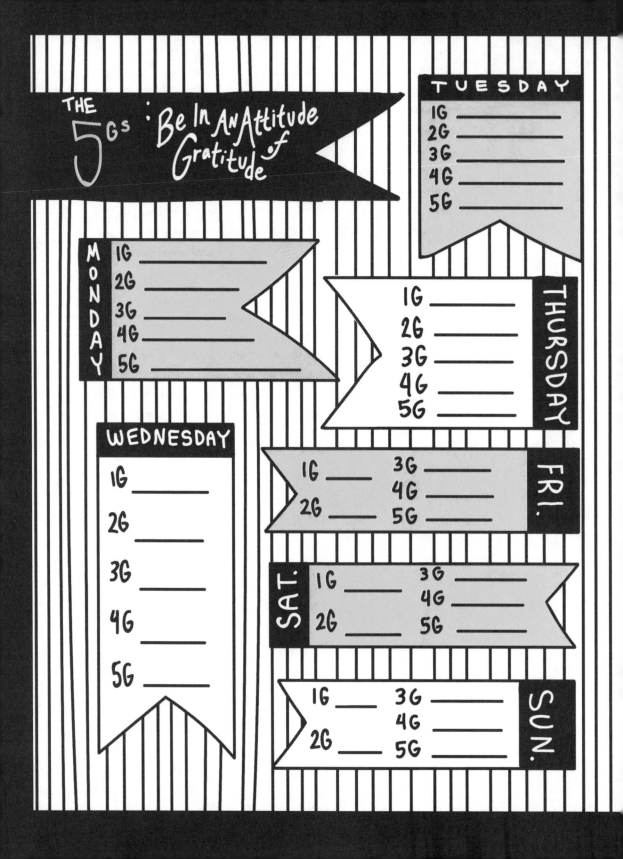

49 : DREAM CATCHER

Living your best life is about having and following your dreams. Dream catchers originated in Native American cultures as a means of spiritual protection for their owners. The dream catcher can attract and catch all sorts of dreams and thoughts into its net or web of fibers. A Native American Hopi proverb says, "All dreams spin out from the same web."

Take in the Good: Take Action

Think about your dreams and aspirations. On the next page, write down your dreams, aspirations, thoughts, and the like on the feathers of your dream catcher. Consider the following areas as inspiration:

- Your relationships—peer, family, romantic
- Your mental and physical health
- Your career
- Your education
- Your freedom
- Your support, security, or stability
- Your desires
- Your wishes
- Your safety
- Your satisfaction
- Your connection

Take in the Good: Takeaway

Life is about dreaming, accomplishing your dreams, and redefining those dreams as you move through the different ages and stages of your life. Billy Mills, the Olympic gold-medal winner and member of the Lakota Sioux tribe said, "Find your dream. It's the pursuit of the dream that heals you."

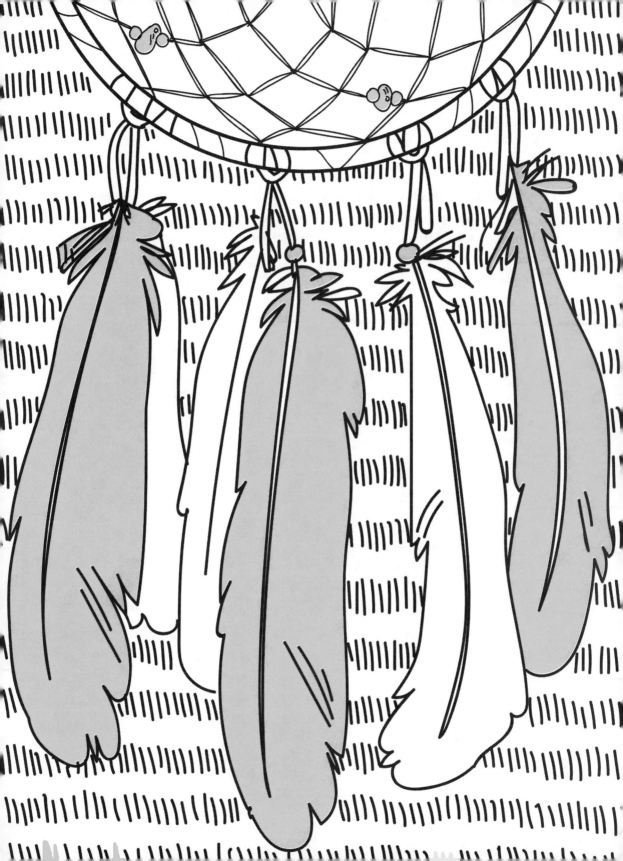

50 : RISE STRONG AND BE A SURVIVOR CREDO

The tools in this book are a guide—the survival gear and compass—for how you can live your best life. Among many other tools, you have learned to take in the good, be a resource for yourself, get your needs met, and be in an attitude of gratitude. You can navigate your days, rise strong, and be a survivor—no matter what life may bring your way.

Take in the Good: Take Action

Read through the credo on the next page for *Rise Strong and Be a Survivor*. While reading the descriptions in the acronym "A SURVIVOR," take mental notes of all the things you have learned for each word.

Now, on the second page, following each word, create your own credo, listing the beliefs or aims that guide you toward living your best life. In the spaces provided, write down what comes to mind when you reflect on the words and what you have learned in this book.

Take in the Good: Takeaway

Use the credo *Rising Strong: You Are a Survivor* as a reminder when you are having a difficult time. Remember to consider your strengths, unique talents, self-respect, values, intuition, heart, and resilience. Rise strong—you are a survivor!

Rise Strong and be A Survivor

CREDO:

RISING STRONG: YOU ARE "A" "SURVIVOR"!

"A"

Awareness: You have learned how to be mindful, spaciously and directly aware. You can choose where to put your attention. You can thoughtfully respond instead of automatically react.

"SURVIVOR"

Strengths: You have many strengths to help you cope and manage painful situations. You can use these strengths to take new paths.

Unique: Don't try to be anyone else. They are already themselves. You are you, with your gifts, flaws, talents, and imperfections. You are, like every human, perfectly imperfect.

Respect: You deserve self-respect and respect from others. Don't let others tear you down. Haters are going to hate. Hang with those who raise you up, not those who tear you down.

Values: Values are the qualities you consider important to you and a way to to live your life. Use these to guide your actions and choices.

Intuition: Trust your gut. Sometimes people can get stuck in their heads. When in doubt, check in with how you feel physically - take a "gut check," and if it doesn't feel right, let this awareness guide your decision-making process and do something different.

Valuable: No one is going to value you as much as you do or can. It is so important to value all the parts of yourself and realize you do, in fact, have value. Self-care is a great way to show yourself how valuable you are. Setting boundaries and saying no are also ways to respect yourself.

Openhearted: Your willingness to share your love and express warm feelings to others and to yourself is important to feel safe, secure, and connected.

Resilience: The ability to bounce back and recover even after adverse and difficult situations, traumas, or tragedies.

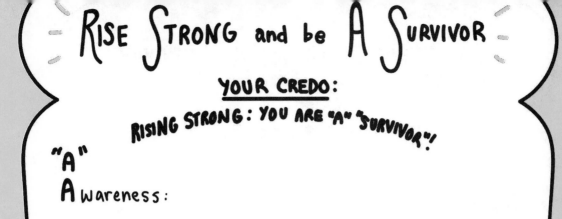

RISE STRONG and be A SURVIVOR

"A"
Awareness:

"SURVIVOR"
Strengths:

Unique:

Respect:

Values:

Intuition

Valuable:

Openhearted:

Resilience: